PORTRAIT
of a
FULFILLED WOMAN

VIRGINIA KIRLEY LEIH

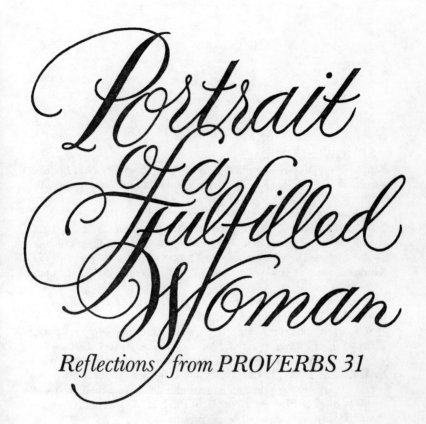

Portrait of a Fulfilled Woman

Reflections from PROVERBS 31

Tyndale House
Publishers, Inc.
Wheaton, Illinois

To Jesus Christ, the Rock for all women and to George, my rock

ACKNOWLEDGMENTS

Scripture quotations identified Berkeley are from *The New Berkeley Version in Modern English*, Zondervan Publishing House, copyright 1969.

Scripture quotations identified *Moffatt* are from *The Bible: A New Translation* by James Moffatt, Copyright 1954 by James A. R. Moffatt.

Scripture quotations identified *New English Bible* are from the *New English Bible* © The Delegates of the Oxford University Press and the Syndics of the Cambridge University Press, 1961 and 1970. Reprinted by permission.

Scripture quotations identified TLB are from *The Living Bible*, Tyndale House Publishers, copyright 1971.

Scripture quotations identified TEV are from the *Good News Bible*, *Today's English Version*, copyright American Bible Society, 1976.

Scripture quotations identified Beck are from *An American Translation* by William F. Becky, Leader Publishing Company, 1976.

Old Testament Scripture quotations identified Amplified are from *Amplified Bible, Old Testament*, copyright 1962, 1964 by Zondervan Publishing House, and are used by permission.

New Testament Scripture quotations identified Amplified are from the *Amplified New Testament* © The Lockman Foundation 1958, and are used by permission.

CONTENTS

ONE
Who Can Find Her?

*Who can find a virtuous woman? for her price
is far above rubies.* Proverbs 31:10

Over the years I've read the Proverbs description of the virtuous
woman often; I've heard it read at bridal showers and women's
meetings—and I've squirmed every time. Because I don't measure up, it always sounds like the impossible dream. For one
thing, I don't even sew!

But the Lord insists that I write about her, and even in these
beginning words, I can only trust him to reveal what he wants
said. He knows better than anyone else my lack of qualifications. But he has reminded me that it was his Spirit that dictated
these words to Lemuel's mother and then to Solomon. He has
told me they weren't meant to be prods, but promises. That
encourages me.

The arresting question, "Who can find her?" introduces this
longest scriptural statement about womanhood, and suggests
that the one who discovers this lovely lady will really strike it rich.

Rubies were the most valuable and costly of precious stones.
The virtuous woman's value is far *above* rubies. Only one other
scriptural term is accorded equal value: wisdom. We can infer
that this woman was wise because she possessed the fear of the
Lord, which is the beginning of wisdom (Psalm 111:10).

But while wisdom is implied, virtue is stated as the all-
encompassing description. I guess I've always thought of virtue

mostly in connection with chastity which involves *not* having committed a particular sin. But I've learned that virtue is really a very positive quality. It's called power, as of an army; worthiness, and valor. Virtue is dynamite!

Vividly the pictures of her life-style flash before us—wool, flax, ships, a vineyard, a candle, tapestry, scarlet, and purple. Personalities are present, too—husband, children, merchants, maids, and the poor.

But does this paragon of womanhood have anything to say to us mortals in this present age? Is she real? Is she credible?

I think yes. I believe that the Holy Spirit inserted this description into God's Word not only because it's a magnificent poem (the first letters of each verse form an alphabetical acrostic in Hebrew) but also because it can be for all of us seekers a manual of instruction and inspiration. This Scripture, too, is profitable.

Further, I believe there's comfort and beauty here for all women, whether or not they wear wedding bands. God has expressed special tenderness for the unmarried, saying he has set them in families. Most single women have households—the office staff, their blood kin, their classrooms, or their churches. They, too, shall be praised.

Written into God's Word are many exciting biographies of women whose lives illustrate the qualities possessed by the Proverbs woman. Like her, each was thoroughly human; and the Holy Spirit selected each story, from among the thousands available, to show us something important about ourselves.

In the many different places we've lived I've been uniquely privileged to know dozens of delightful, dedicated Christian women. The flashes of Godlikeness (for we were created in his image and then recreated in Christ Jesus) that I have seen in these, my friends, have marvelously illuminated my own walk. Poet Luci Shaw expresses beautifully what I have so often felt.

SALUTATION [1]
(St. Luke 1:39–45)

Framed in light,
Mary sings through the doorway.
Elizabeth's six month joy
jumps, a palpable greeting,
a hidden first encounter
between son and Son.

And my heart turns over
when I meet Jesus
in you.

[1] Reprinted from *The Secret Trees*, by Luci Shaw, © 1976, Harold Shaw Publishers, Box 567, Wheaton, Illinois 60187. Used by permission.

TWO
A Husband's Heart Trusts

*The heart of her husband doth safely trust in
her, so that he shall have no need of spoil.*
Proverbs 31:11

From far above rubies to a husband's heart is an arresting
transition. But that's where the marriage begins—and that's
where it continues. No cheap sentimentality, this—for his
"heart" includes his think-about and his aim-to-do, as well as his
want-to.

When I was a bride, the Lord carefully exposed me to Max
and Thelma in Omaha. Often during Wednesday night's testimony time, Max would rise, his brown face shining: "I thank
the Lord for saving me and for giving me this wonderful wife."
Fondly he would pat the shoulder of the quiet, brown-haired
woman by his side.

Thelma, who grew up in Kansas, and Max, a Filipino, met at
Bible school and then married. Forty years ago those things
weren't done much. Even Christians were critical. When the
children came, dark like their father, called "nigger" sometimes,
or otherwise rejected, Thelma's rare courage and gentle wisdom
made it right. Max trusted her, you see, with all his heart; and
that (as Frost said) made all the difference.

On the other hand, my grandfather married his first be-
trothed only to believe that the first baby came too soon to be his
own. Then one evening when he came home from work, the
baby was dead. Suspecting that his wife had killed the baby in

10

order to keep him, he divorced her. Today I hurt for that dead baby and for the fearful, cast-off girl—but mostly for the man who could not trust his wife.

"Doth safely trust. . . ." The Hebrew uses a redundancy here, the same root word twice, like saying "trustfully trusts." It must be important.

I believe that the ability to commit, to put all the eggs into one basket, in marriage, is a gift our Lord will give to partners who are united in his will and who ask him for it.

The Maker, who is the Husband to all women, is a Truster. He trusted his only Son to a rotten world, knowing he would be crucified, and gave all things into his son's hand.

The Son, in turn, will trust to us the very essence of himself, the Holy Spirit to become resident in us. Knowing how earthen is my vessel, he trusts me even with the delicate task of bringing the gospel to my neighbor, who can see my backyard and observe my children.

I think God wants to give husbands trusting hearts so that they, like Christ, may give themselves for their wives. It's a terrible vulnerability.

The story of the Shunammite woman's husband always moves me. Not only did he send his ailing son at once to his mother, but when she, following the child's death, asked her husband for transportation to the prophet, he promptly granted it. It's true that he didn't understand why she needed to go to meeting when there wasn't any. But when he heard his wife say, "It will be all right" (2 Kings 4:23, Amplified), he accepted her word with simple trust; and his son became his heir.

The Bible attaches a startling reward to trusting: the husband will have no need of spoil. Will trusting one's wife really immunize a man against the temptation to cheat on his income tax, or steal his employer's lumber, or make personal long distance calls on the company's charge? Has anyone done a study on the correlation between trust and honesty? Will the wife's providence remove the pressure for her husband to be dishonest?

God's Word is full of intriguing possibilities.

THREE
She Does Him Good

*She will do him good and not evil all the days of
her life.* Proverbs 31:12

During our first year of marriage and mine of teaching, George,
then in premedical studies, said one day, "You must try for a job
in South Dakota because we need to move there so I can get into
medical school."

Now I liked Colorado, where we were living, especially my
very first job in Swink. And I didn't like South Dakota. I'd grown
up there during grasshopper invasions which blanketed houses,
and dust storms so fierce that one day in our kitchen the bread
my mother buttered me grew black and the dirt gritted in my
teeth before I could finish half a slice. I much preferred mountains, waterfalls, and blue spruce, thank you.

Furthermore, I'd been an honor graduate and a debate
champion. Who was this South Dakota boy to tell me what to do?
So I said no. (I'd never heard of submission!)

But George carefully repeated his case. "Medical school
applicants are swarming now since the end of World War Two.
The only chance I have of being accepted is to try for a resident's
preference."

Troubled, I wrote an S.O.S. to my college professor, advisor,
and mentor, dear Dr. Culver. "An *intelligent* woman," this unmarried lady replied, "chooses what is best for her husband."

Well—put that way—I decided on South Dakota!

12

One Sunday evening while Thelma waited for Max and their children, she and I visited on the varnished, splintery wooden pews. I remember her statement: "A wife should never criticize her husband. He is, after all, the one she chose." I needed to hear that, too.

Years later I read, "Every wise woman builds her house, but the foolish one tears it down with her own hands" (Proverbs 14:1, Amp.).

Certainly I've heard many women tear down with their tongues as they ticked off their husbands' faults. Do men criticize their wives when they're talking together? I'm afraid it's a more commonly female failing.

Perhaps that's why, after a husband's trust, the wife's set of mind and course of action is described: "She will do him good and not evil all the days of her life" (Proverbs 31:12).

I love to read about Abigail who acted for her husband when he didn't even know it. Nabal was a fool and he insulted David. So David set out with 400 armed men, and he wasn't planning a picnic. Abigail, who was both beautiful and wise, met the troops and fell at David's feet. With consummate diplomacy, she acknowledged her husband's gross behavior, taking upon herself his iniquity, and begged to serve David and his crew. (She just happened to have along enough bread, mutton, wine, corn, and raisins for the army, plus fig cakes for dessert!) It turned out to be a picnic after all.

God himself later took care of Nabal. Meanwhile Abigail stood between her husband and the wrath of David. Eventually she became David's wife, riding in state this time upon a donkey, with five maids in waiting. I think the Lord is trying to tell us something. Did you know that he's planning for all of us to become the bride of a King?

There's another lovely husband-wife relationship implied in the story of Samson's parents. To the barren wife of Manoah appeared an angel with the good news that she would have a son. The requirement for her and for their son, the angel said, was to abstain from wine and unclean food; and the son was never to cut his hair.

Excitedly Mrs. Manoah recounted the experience to her husband—if they are finally going to have a child, he should, of course, be the first to know—sharing with him the spiritual nature of her experience as she described the man with a countenance like an angel.

Manoah's reaction was interesting. He asked God for a rerun so that they could obtain more information about how to teach the coming child.

God obliged, but again the angel came to the woman alone. Determined to include her husband this time, she asked the angel to wait while she ran for Manoah.

The third act involves all three players, with Manoah in the role of interrogator. First he made sure this was the same "man" who had come earlier, and then he asked him how they should manage the child.

The angel answered politely, although he said nothing new, only, "Be sure that your wife follows the instructions I gave her" (Judges 13:13, TLB). (Evidently husbands are to help their wives obey God's orders even if they didn't hear them being given.)

Perhaps Manoah thought to learn more if he could just keep that man a while longer, so he asked him to stay for dinner. Still courteous, the angel agreed. "I won't eat," he said, "but you may give a burnt offering to the Lord."

Again Manoah's insatiable curiosity surfaced and he asked the man's name. (He explained that he wanted to be able to give the proper credit when the prediction was fulfilled.) This time the angel parried with his own question: "Why do you ask My name, seeing it is wonderful?" (Judges 13:18, Amp.).

He must have been the pre-incarnate Jesus!

Then comes the awesome climax. In the flame of fire from the burnt offering the man ascended into heaven, and Manoah and his wife fell on their faces to the ground. Although his wife had tried to convey the fact, Manoah finally recognized that he had been associating with the supernatural!

All of a sudden the intellectual cravings of Manoah dissolved in terror, and he voiced the primitive fear that having seen God, they would certainly die. We can only imagine the effect this divine display must have had on a couple who had never seen the Wonderful World of Disney.

At that point Mrs. Manoah's practical wisdom balanced her husband's analytical probing, and she "did him good." But oh, so tactfully! Basing her argument on the revealed character of God, she gently refuted: "If the Lord were going to kill us he wouldn't have accepted our burnt offerings and wouldn't have appeared to us and told us this wonderful thing and done these miracles" (Judges 13:23, TLB).

I was grieved once as I listened to one ill older woman, only weeks before her death, continue in her habit of denouncing her husband, who himself died just a few months later. He did have faults, but I thought that if she had done him good, "and not evil," they might both have had many more years of life— happily.

When my parents first began attending church, our family met Jennie Lindbloom, a blind woman whose constant spirit of praise to God and of loving appreciation for the thoughtfulness of her husband Axel greatly influenced my father to desire to know her Savior.

Many years later, not long after our marriage, George and I visited this couple, now in their old age. Axel held Jennie's hand as they sat side by side and said, "The Lord has been so good to give us so many years together. For so long I had to be Mama's eyes. But now I am deaf, and I need Mama, whose hearing is still very good, to be my ears."

Jennie smiled with the special childlike radiance of the un-sighted, and I realized how pleased she was to be able to do her husband good "all the days of her life."

Besides polishing his image for our children and others, I'm trying to understand better how to do my husband good. Recently I rearranged the bedroom furniture as he had suggested. Today I have prayed for him and with him. Tonight I plan to broil the hamburgers, although I hate to scour the broiler, because he isn't supposed to eat fried foods. And when I go shopping, I'll try to remember that he needs dental ribbon (not floss), unwaxed.

When I run out of good things to do, I can always meditate on 1 Peter 3:2 in *The Amplified Bible*, where I am told to " . . . respect, defer to, revere him; to honor, esteem, appreciate, prize and adore him; to admire, praise, be devoted to, deeply love and enjoy" my husband. Likely it will take a day or two for me to implement those orders.

He does have his faults. He has a thing about locking doors, which is irritating as I fumble for the key and balance grocery bags. He's always stopping to take pictures when we travel, and he constantly buys books. But I won't be perfect myself until next year.

And he trusts me.

FOUR
She Works Willingly

*She seeketh wool, and flax, and worketh
willingly with her hands.* Proverbs 31:13

The Proverbs lady is practical. Having decided to do her husband only good (Jesus, too, "went about doing good"), she sets out to provide for a basic need, clothing. She doesn't look in the ready-to-wear department but goes for the raw materials, wool and flax. For her time that covered the options: animal and vegetable sources, one for winter and one for summer.

The Lord God made the lambs and started the flax to growing. (He also started the garment industry!) But he depends on us to get the wool from the sheep's backs to ours and the flax from field to fellow.

When I was very small, I craved above all else to wash dishes like Mother. My cowboy daddy took time to make a small wooden stool so I could reach the enamel dishpan on the pull-out shelf of our Hoover cabinet, and on the appointed day I got up at 5 A.M. to be sure I wouldn't miss out. Mother let me roll and squish the bar of P & G into the hot water to make suds—what fun!—and then she even let me wash the fragile kerosene lamp chimneys—first, while the water was cleanest.

How gracious of God to let us be *his* helpers!

Making clothing reminds me of barren, battered Hannah. As if the hollow hurting in her own childless breast was not enough, she was tormented by fertile Peninnah, the other wife; misunderstood by her husband (who thought he was worth more than ten sons, bless his loving male chauvinist heart); and maligned even by Priest Eli who couldn't read lips well enough to discern that she wasn't drunk.

Hannah drove a hard bargain, then, with God himself—hard for her, surely—giving back to the Lord the longed-for son when he was just a little lad. Her mother arms were empty again. Ah, but the mother hands stayed busy. Annually, the Spirit records, Hannah made Samuel a little coat and took it to him when she went to church.

Each year Hannah calculated how much bigger Samuel would have grown. And even though God gave her five more children, he also allowed her to participate in the life of her firstborn—who was her nation's first prophet—by clothing him with her own love-wrought stitches. (See 1 Samuel 1; 2:18, 19.)

There's something in us women that longs to do for those we love. Jesus knew about this—he was with the Father when it was invented and installed—and so he joyfully accepted feminine ministry. It was the *hand* of Peter's mother-in-law that he touched. Did he understand how much she wanted to be able to serve her guests?

Jesus even *asked* for a drink of water from the woman of Samaria, startling her prejudice, peeling off the layered scar tissue of flippancy, sarcasm, and evasiveness so that he might open old infected wounds and bathe them in living water.

Perhaps this compelling desire to minister found its ultimate expression in grieving Mary Magdalene, who yearned to anoint the dead body of her Lord, apparently not realizing that Mary of Bethany's alabaster had already taken care of that. Thus, first in all history, she came face to face with the risen Christ, and breathed "Rabboni!" (John 20:16).

I think God means for us to seek our "wool and flax" by helping us to define the raw materials of our trade. That seems kind of obvious, but it's easy to miss. When I was a teacher, I tried to remember what I'd been taught—I was to teach kids, not English. But when I became a full-time mother, I forgot that principle. One day my usually pleasant first toddler was demanding and difficult. Her interruptions hindered me and I grew increasingly frustrated until the time my husband came home, when I exclaimed, "Becky has been so difficult today that she has interfered with my work!"

George's reply went straight to the mark: "Becky *is* your work."

If the secretary's wool and flax is words per minute, she can seek more of them. Whatever their chief occupation, modern women today require many qualities: efficiency, craftsmanship, creativity, knowledge, and stamina. These and more our Father is pleased to have us seek.

Our raw material may sometimes appear to us to be very skimpy. A life of eighty-four years of widowhood, spent in an enclosure smaller than a city block, doesn't seem terribly significant. But when it was developed by worship and fasting and prayer, it eventually put Anna the prophetess in the right place at the right time to meet Infant Divinity, and gave her something to talk about to all who would listen.

The developing, the working willingly—that's our part. For God is interested in excellence. (Jesus not only went about doing good, but he did everything well!) That's what the Proverbs lady was after.

I once knew of a Sunday school class called Willing Workers. Being one never appealed to me very much. I could only imagine a household menial with inferior mental equipment (why else would she be willing?) drudging away at some dreary chore like scouring garbage pails.

Then I discovered that working willingly is scriptural. The Hebrew "worketh" used in this phrase means to accomplish in the broadest sense, to bestow, bring forth, finish, and fulfill. "Willingly" derives from the noun, "pleasure," carrying the idea of delight. The Proverbs lady was absolutely hilarious about accomplishing things.

So I've had to revise my estimate of a willing worker and ask the Lord to make me one. My mother is one—all four feet and ten inches of her. Washday, when I was growing up, was horrendous. Hand-hauled water steamed and sizzled in copper boilers (worth $50 and up, now, in antique shops) on the black kitchen range. Sorted laundry mounded the kitchen floor. After extending the exhaust hose through a window, Mother mashed down on the foot starter of our gasoline Maytag, and its chugging filled our small frame house. If my sisters and I weren't already up, Mother snatched the sheets for the first load out from under us while we giggled and protested. (Mother always believed in getting a very early start.) We knew the same thing would happen to our pajamas if we weren't dressed in time for the colored load. It was years before I ever heard the term "blue Monday." My mother, now approaching eighty, still has fun working.

Sometimes it seems I have to work a long time on my wool and flax without seeing results. A few of my friends, whose problems I have so *clearly* pointed out, still make occasional mistakes. Even my kids, with whom I started from scratch, daily reveal imperfections. Is it a vitamin deficiency which keeps them from wanting to clean their rooms or write thank-you letters? And I, whose recurring prayer has been, "Lord, you stopped the lions' mouths; please shut mine also when necessary," still have attacks of verbitis.

But the Lord shows me now that I am not to be discouraged. I am required only to be a seeker and a developer and processor. I am not to fret over what I see in the darkroom as I work. God took the original picture. He will perfect it in his image—and in his time. Hallelujah!

FIVE
She Brings Food from Afar

She is like the merchants' ships; she bringeth her food from afar. She riseth also while it is yet night, and giveth meat to her household, and a portion to her maidens.
Proverbs 31:14, 15

The other basic need with which the Proverbs woman is involved is food for her household. An intriguing picture of her zest is "like the merchants' ships." These were vessels which scurried from port to port in their trading ventures.

God is interested in what we eat, having provided in the first garden everything that was good for food; in the books of the Law, several recipes for the uses of meat; and in the wilderness, angels' food for his wandering children.

Jesus, who regularly taught God's extension courses, made water into wine at Cana, bread and fish into lots more of the same—with leftovers—for 5,000; and nothing at all into fifty-three fish whose weight didn't burst the nets. One of my favorite examples of tender thoughtfulness is the breakfast cookout by the Sea of Tiberius prepared by the risen Christ for his sleepless, hungry, and errant disciples.

Ruth went into the fields to glean grain. There she found not only an ephah of barley, but a husband—and the right to wear the family crest of the Lion of the tribe of Judah.

Today's supermarket shelves carry more than our wallets can afford. It doesn't seem likely that this passage enjoins us to become gadding gourmets hunting expensive edibles. But our quest might well take us "backwards" to find what is genuinely nutritious. A mother, whose story is told in the February 1977 issue of *Christian Life* magazine, has done that and compiled her results into the *Old Fashioned Recipe Book.* Many other authors are currently telling us of the importance of proper food.

But I think God also wants us to consider food as any kind of needed nourishment for those in our redemptive circle.

One day I was lonely and so I prayed, "Jesus, please let me hear that someone cares."

The following morning a new friend phoned: "Virginia, I just want to tell you that I love you." Suddenly my day sparkled. My friend was also gladdened to learn that she had answered a prayer, and we both dined on the golden apples of a word fitly spoken.

"Afar" in the Hebrew connotes breadth and liberty. The Proverbs woman did not overlook unlikely sources of nourishment.

One day a suffering mother phoned me. Her teenage son, angry about parental restrictions, had stormed away from home. The hot words exchanged continued to ring in my friend's ears. We prayed, committing the boy to the God who knows all about rebellion, and asked that "laborers" be sent to him. Several days later when he returned, calmer and wiser, he told his astonished mother that somewhere in California, alone and out of steam, he met two young Mormon missionaries who talked with him a long time and helped him get his head together. That mother had not expected the Lord to work that way, but she was much too wise to knock it.

I'm not sure why affluent Lydia went to her riverside prayer group to worship on the rocky beach instead of to some more proper or comfortable place. But I do read that she heard Paul there, that the Lord opened her heart, and that she requested not only baptism for herself and household but also that the evangelists be her house guests.

We don't have to be hung up on our own concepts of orthodoxy. God can speak in any way he chooses—through the wrath of men, a corrupt high priest named Caiaphas, or Balaam's donkey! Liberty is the lingering fragrance which identifies the Spirit of the Lord.

And yet on our part that liberty comes only through the truth which makes us free; consequently the Word admonishes us to hold sound doctrine and specifically warns us to avoid what is spiritually destructive.

Hazel's life read like a classic tragedy. Beginning with a difficult stepmother, it continued with several marriages, an attempted suicide, and the giving up of her only child for adoption. Her life nearly ended with the murder of her last, beloved husband while he was away philandering. But she became a beautiful woman, a skilled artist, and a constant searcher for the reality of the God-glimmerings which came to her as a little girl, such as her vision of angel-writing on the sand at dawn.

One night God gave her a vision of Jesus, complete except for his face, and she was never again the same. "I had a sense of total well-being," she said. So at a Billy Graham crusade, while George Beverly Shea sang "How Great Thou Art," she gave her heart to that Jesus.

Several years later she heard about the Holy Spirit and was gloriously indwelt by him. She declared, "There is more of this, but none Other." Hazel gave all her extensive library of occult books to be burned.

Like all the rest of God's children, however, she did not achieve instant perfection. Though we in her fellowship urged her to study the Scriptures, she continued to read, instead, whatever caught her eye on the bookstore shelves. One day she stopped at my house, weeping, having just read a book purporting to show that the sayings of Jesus were not original with him but had been acquired during hidden years among the Essenes. "I've staked my life on him!" she cried. "Now what?"

I'd been gentle with Hazel, but suddenly I was exasperated with her and thoroughly angry at our adversary, the devil. "Hazel," I exploded, "you're committing spiritual pornography!"

She was momentarily stunned. Then she quavered, "But aren't we supposed to know the truth?"

"You *have* the truth," I answered. "Jesus Christ is the Truth, and his Holy Spirit, who lives in you, is the Spirit of Truth!" Then as we prayed together, our Father was plenteous in mercy to forgive and comfort.

My friend Margaret, on the other hand, is a highly educated, much-traveled, and anointed woman who must presently serve in a religious institution where she feels spiritually stifled. Although she is a loyal, agreeing member of her denomination, her heart cries out in that place for his freedom. I suspect that thousands of God's women operate within restrictive situations, gasping for the fresh breath of the Spirit which sustains the spirit.

For such persons the food from afar may require an intensive rather than an extensive search, one which the Father has repeatedly promised to reward.

Psalm 34:8 encourages us to "taste . . . the Lord is good." In his "show and tell" with the loaves and fishes, Jesus declared that he is the bread of heaven upon which we can feed. David exclaimed, "How sweet are Your words to my taste, sweeter than honey to my mouth" (Psalm 119:103, Amp.).

Before my two youngest were in school but after they had outgrown naps, I found myself, like many mothers, with very little time alone. During the evenings I wanted to be with my husband and school-age daughter and needed to catch up on housework. (I discovered that if I mopped the kitchen floor after the children went to bed, it stayed clean all night!) But my inner resources needed shoring up more than ever. The Lord had recently given me a new, special love for his Word, but I needed time to explore it and visit with its Author.

The obvious solution was rising earlier, but I couldn't set the alarm without disturbing my husband, and getting up early was not one of my natural talents. So, remembering that the Lord wakened Isaiah morning by morning, I told the Lord that if he would do that for me, I would pray and study his Word.

God was disconcertingly prompt. The very next morning my

eyelids flew open at 4:30. "Lord," I complained, "wouldn't 5:30 have been soon enough? You know I'm a rapid reader."

But I didn't dare go back to sleep, so I stumbled out to the kitchen, made a cup of coffee, and at the kitchen table plunged into the Word. Thus began a most beautiful communion with the Lord. Starting with Proverbs, which previously I had not paid much attention to, I found how smart—and how contemporary—God is. I was astonished to read that the wounds of a friend, which for me right then were really hurting, are better than the kisses of an enemy. I delighted in his humor: "As a ring of gold in a swine's snout, so is a fair woman who is without discretion" (Proverbs 11:22, Amp.). I discovered that "good news nourishes the bones," and my husband pointed out that bones are important because the blood is manufactured in them.

Then the Lord started to awaken me with a portion of Scripture or phrase of a song which was to be exactly, and sometimes desperately, needed for that day. Because I was being fed the finest of the wheat, I not only looked forward to our morning trysts, but I began taking Word snacks throughout the day.

One evening I read, "Fear not, but let your hands be strong and hardened" (Zechariah 8:13, Amp.). That sounded as if trouble was coming, so I was not surprised at a phone call the next day from a weeping friend whose mate wanted to dissolve their marriage.

My love for these friends was great, so I began to haunt the Scriptures, sometimes hourly, to learn how to pray for them. Repeatedly the Holy Spirit brought me to verses of encouragement, such as "[Love] is ever ready to believe the best of every person, its hopes are fadeless under all circumstances" (1 Corinthians 13:7, Amp.), or "For with God nothing shall be impossible" (Luke 1:37). God healed the marriage, and he taught me how to intercede even as his Word fed me.

About that time I realized that the Lord was serious about wanting me to write. I enrolled at the local university with a writing instructor who was not initially impressed with my efforts. Though I was really tempted to drop the course, I continued to work hard and eventually learned a great deal from my professor. At the end of the semester, as I approached the completion of an article for publication, I was suddenly flooded with a joy like none I had ever before experienced. I felt like dancing and I didn't even know how! Trying to analyze the reason for such heavenly elixir, I remembered the words of Jesus, "My meat is to do the will of him who sent me" (John 4:34). The will of God was feeding me, and it was indescribably delicious.

God's Word, Jesus himself, the Father's will—these we can rise to obtain while still it is dark.

And then we can give them to our households.

Priscilla, of New Testament splendor, had that privilege. Apollos came by on tour one day, and though he possessed a golden tongue and great boldness, his knowledge was incomplete. Priscilla and husband Aquila made him a temporary member of their household and fed him a massive diet supplement: "the way of God more perfectly" (Acts 18:26).

Finally, our Proverbs lady assigned her maids their tasks. This gives me hope. I don't have to feed everybody all by myself! I tend to want to program and prescribe for everyone. That's probably why Paul told Timothy to "Teach these great truths to trustworthy men who will, in turn, pass them on to others" (2 Timothy 2:2, TLB) . . . and why wise Jethro gave Moses a specific design for delegating authority (Exodus 18). (In-laws can be useful!) God's plan works. After being nourished by Priscilla and Aquila, Apollos zipped over to Greece where his zeal became power as he proved to the Jews by the Word that Jesus is the Christ.

It's a high privilege—to assign portions—even if we can't afford maids. My friend Barbara, a beautiful minister's wife who often speaks to women, says it's time we ladies enjoyed the many things Scripture says we can do rather than to chafe over what seems to be prohibited. One of the can-do's, she points out, is for older women to "train the younger women to . . . love their husbands and their children" (Titus 2:4, TLB). The younger women, then, have pass-along privileges to their children.

I was scrubbing the bathroom one hot Oklahoma day when

my five-year-old son came indoors with his little sister to inquire, "Mommy, why did God make mosquitoes?" Now that hints at heavy theology—leading to the origin of evil—but as I sat on the floor with one hand dripping in the commode, I did my best to explain. I remember being very thankful that I was immediately available to teach the ones most precious to me.

And at this moment I am full-heartedly grateful that there is so much for me to enjoy, distribute, and commit to others of the "fathomless wealth of Christ" (Ephesians 3:8, Berkeley).

SIX
She Considers a Field

She considereth a field, and buyeth it: with the
fruit of her hands she planteth a vineyard.
Proverbs 31:16

So far our Proverbs lady has been pretty much a doer. Now she emerges also as a thinker. She is looking over a piece of land which she considers buying. The verb "consider" used here means to plot, plan, scheme, or devise. She's thinking on all of her cylinders!

A few years ago when we wished we owned property, my husband read this passage, peered at me over his glasses, and demanded, "When are you going to buy a field?"

Few of us today are in the market for land. But all of us women are investors. It's where we choose to sink our funds that demands scrutiny.

Just after one of our moves, I met a young woman who evidently liked me at once. Soon she was at my house for tea and stayed four hours. I shared Jesus with her, and she seemed interested. She began taking lots of my time, and I didn't mind (it's fun to be liked), especially if I could help her. But when I started feeling uneasy about the relationship, I sought counsel from my friend Myrtie, a New Testament kind of saint and careful student of the Scriptures. As we prayed together, the Lord brought to Myrtie's attention this phrase, "consider the field."

"I am inclined to think," Myrtie said, "that this field may not be so productive as others you might 'buy.' Ask the Lord and he will show you."

I was gradually able to understand, then, that my young friend was more interested in an intimate and time-consuming friendship than she was in knowing God better. The Lord himself rearranged our circumstances so that snubs were not necessary, and we remained comfortable with each other.

Then he showed me a different field. George and I spent an afternoon with Sandy, a realtor with whom I felt instant rapport. As she drove us over the city, I realized that she was deeply troubled. And as I later thought of her, I felt strongly that I should try to visit with her. With surprised pleasure she accepted my invitation for a restaurant lunch. When the subject of church arose, she inquired about my affiliation. We didn't yet have a church home, but I could and did talk about the Lord Jesus. He gave me great freedom as I shared his love and goodness.

Sandy believed what I told her, for that very morning she had begged God for guidance concerning a major decision. She hadn't been to church for a dozen years, ever since a deacon took her little girls' Sunday school class away from her because she smoked (he smoked, too, she said, but not when anyone was looking). Instead of attending church, she had talked to the Lord during long walks among the sagebrush and scrub cedar.

Again, weeks later, we had lunch. Her problem had not been solved, but I urged her to turn it, and herself, over to the Problem-taker. A few days later I received her note: "On the way back to the office, just before the Abriendo exit at twelve minutes until 12:00, I had the greatest urge to say, 'Yes, dear Lord, take my life and do with it as you will.' I just felt so relieved and unburdened. At the office my boss said, 'You look as though you've had a great experience.' I told him I had and could handle things now, thanks to God's help."

I saw Sandy for the third and last time when we thought we might need a temporary rental. Because I was weak from a lengthy bout with flu, she offered to come to our house. After business, she shared over coffee her concerns about her children. I asked if we might pray for them, and then I voiced our petitions to the Father. When she rose to leave, she said to me with tears, "Virginia, may I hug you?"

Now I was anything but huggable in my grungy bathrobe and uncurled hair, but that brief embrace felt so very good, warming my heart and giving me tangible, needed strength for that day.

Recently Sandy wrote that she is living for the Lord and happier than she ever thought possible. I suppose I spent not more than five hours with her, but she was a fertile field, indeed—and I loved her.

I am *not* suggesting that God intends us to look over our list of acquaintances and play "eeny, meeny," accepting or rejecting according to whim. The gracious woman has an initially accepting spirit toward every person. The first young woman was every bit as worthwhile to our Father as the second—and for someone else her field may have produced a bumper crop—but she was not my assignment at that time.

Fields are not always people. Sometimes they are projects, or committees, or potlucks, or being convention delegates—or any one of numerous activities, some delightful and some difficult. The only way I know to properly sort out what fields we should or should not buy is to rely on the promised guidance of the Holy Spirit who will, Jesus said, teach us all things. Our considering is only complete with him.

Shortly after we had become his parishioners, Pastor Dave phoned me one day: "Virginia, as I have prayed about someone to share in one of our services, you have come to mind. Will you also pray about it and let me know?" What a marvelous request! It allowed me freedom in Christ to consider the field.

I have tried to make it a policy to say "yes" or "no" to a proffered responsibility only after I have truly "considered." But sometimes I forget. Very recently someone approached me about becoming president of a local club. My natural self instantly recoiled, and I blurted, "Oh, no, I'm still too new to the community!" When I reached home, the Holy Spirit gently and firmly reproached me. So I needed to phone the lovely lady who asked the question—yes, I think I had hurt her—and apologize, explaining that my answer should have been, "I'll pray about it."

Queen Vashti, Esther's predecessor, considered a field, the request of a drunken king who showed off his kingdom in a profligate, 180-day bash, and then, in defiance of existing standards of womanly modesty, wanted to show her off. She rejected it. It was an expensive decision, costing her the queenship and perhaps her head.

But Vashti's honorable choice made it possible for Esther the Jewess to survey her field, mined as it was with treachery, intrigue, and peril, and to accept it. When Esther declared, "And so will I go in unto the king, which is not according to the law: and if I perish, I perish" (Esther 4:16), she bought the preservation of a nation, protecting the ancestors of Jesus Christ.

Checking out the options, and then ascertaining what God wants, becomes not only a matter of personal peace, but also of efficiency. The *Amplified Bible* translates Proverbs 31:16: "She considers a new field before she buys or accepts it—expanding prudently [and not courting neglect of her present duties by assuming others]. With her savings [of time and strength] she plants fruitful vines in her vineyard."

Because the Proverbs woman chose carefully, her field turned over enough profit for her to plant a vineyard. But vineyards promise neither quick returns nor easy money. Grapes don't grow until at least two years after planting, and constant pruning and cultivating are necessary to keep the vines producing. The lady was patient! And the vines were fruitful.

With each of my three babies there came a morning when I awoke, realizing that I had not gotten up for a 2 A.M. feeding because my infant had slept the entire night. Therein I greatly rejoiced, deciding, *It is a human being after all*!

I confess to moments of doubt since. Last week I read a news release on a National Institute on Education study of seventh graders. The researcher concluded that the seventh grade is the most difficult school year between grades one and twelve—for students, teachers, and parents. The reviewer suggested a label: "Warning: The seventh grade may be hazardous to your health." My husband and I have just lived through two seventh graders in a row, and the man is right!

But a few months ago when I was agonizing over one of our children, the Lord directed me to Luke 8:15, which tells of the good ground where those with an honest and good heart keep the word and bring forth fruit with patience. Very emphatically the Lord reassured me that this child *is* good ground, in which we have planted the good seed with prayer and all the wisdom we could acquire. He promised me that with patience we *would* bring forth fruit. Since then we've seen some beautiful glimpses of the ripening product.

I believe that whether we're raising kids or doing something else, God wants us to believe in the ultimate fruitfulness of our vineyards, and that even in these times of instant everything, we are capable of learning his patience.

Besides, we have his promise: "Since future victory is sure, be strong and steady, always abounding in the Lord's work, for you know that nothing you do for the Lord is ever wasted. . . ." (1 Corinthians 15:58, TLB).

Hallelujah, once again!

SEVEN
She Strengthens Herself

*She girdeth her loins with strength, and
strengtheneth her arms.* Proverbs 31:17

Up to this point we've seen the Proverbs woman in relation to
her husband, her household, her servants, and her projects.
Now we come to the way she treats herself. Because she is wise,
she has a healthy regard for her own needs as a person. First
mentioned is her realization that she can use strength, and I can
relate to that!

Characteristically vivid is the picture of a woman putting on
strength as she would a girdle, for "loins" refers to the small
of the back. All of us who have bent over typewriters or stood
behind counters for eight-hour shifts, or who have carried growing babies know how painfully fatigue can strike that part
of our bodies.

The strength with which she girds is synonymous with force,
security, majesty, and boldness. The lady actively puts this power
upon herself—she doesn't wait for it to happen.

After taking care of her back so that she can stand (reminis-
cent of the "stand therefore" in the "whole armor" description in
Ephesians), the Spirit says she strengthens her arms. This
"strengthen" refers to being alert either physically or mentally,
either courageous or hardened. And the arms refer to the
stretched-out limbs, implying force and strength. Thus by the

33

use of these rich words, Scripture shows us a woman seeking to apply power for bold outreach or steadfast endurance.

"Lord," I asked as I pondered this passage yesterday, "what example do you want me to use? Who was the strongest woman in the Bible?"

As I waited prayerfully, he gave me a surprising answer: "Mary, the mother of Jesus."

I had studied Mary, although not with strength in mind, so with excitement I turned to the beginning of Luke's Gospel. I saw that although Mary was at first troubled by the angel's appearance and then puzzled about the manner by which the announced birth would occur, she exhibited many kinds of strength.

The first was the strength of submission to the known will of God: "Be it unto me according to thy word" (Luke 1:38). Even then, she must have been aware of the risks involved in showing up pregnant before the marriage was consummated. Probably she expected to lose Joseph as well as respectability, and knew that she might legally be stoned. It was a courageous submission.

Next, Mary sought the strength of fellowship. She went immediately to her relative Elizabeth who, having experienced the miracle of conception in old age, was uniquely qualified to stand with Mary in her miraculous but precarious situation. It was the angel Gabriel who told Mary about Elizabeth's condition, but Mary's own bright-eyed intelligence and initiative propelled her to Elizabeth's fellowship in the hill country.

Queen Esther also sought the fellowship of her maids to fast with her before she approached the king. And after Daniel had received the impossible assignment of interpreting a dream which King Nebuchadnezzar had forgotten, he went to his house and asked his three friends to pray with him.

Years later Mary was to keep company with yet other women—Mary Magdalene and Mary the wife of Cleopas—as she stood at the cross, where, as Simeon had prophesied, the sword pierced her own soul also.

Then Mary experienced the strength of revelation. She could not produce that, of course, but she could and did set in motion the circumstances which made it possible. Something far more powerful than nuclear reaction passed between Mary and Elizabeth at Mary's greeting. Not only did John the Baptist leap in Elizabeth's womb, but Mary heard Elizabeth echo Gabriel's words, "Blessed art thou among women," and knew that only the Lord himself could have revealed them. (She hadn't even had time yet to tell Elizabeth her news.) If, as she traveled, Mary had any temptation to dismiss the whole matter as a hallucination, Elizabeth's impassioned utterance must have given her complete reassurance of its reality. Part of the strength of revelation for Mary was the sense of God's delighted approval of her, for he moved Elizabeth to declare, "Blessed is she that believed" (Luke 1:45a). (We, too, delight our Lord when we accept what he says.)

A few years ago as my husband neared the end of his residency in psychiatry, he started searching for (as we both prayed earnestly about) his practice location. Eventually the choice narrowed to two, both of which he visited, and he decided on the one in Oregon. As we began to plan, however, I became increasingly uneasy about that choice and talked a great deal to the Lord about it—though I tried not to influence George. (Years later I was to read the following explicit paragraph in a booklet by Shade Driscoll: "The matter of a man's work is between him and the Lord. Where he works and what he does is decided by his Maker, not by his wife. God took Adam and put him in the garden to dress and keep it before Eve was even made!"[1])

A strange thing occurred. The Oregon group failed to acknowledge George's letter of acceptance and a secretary sent him, instead, a large portfolio of literature as if he were just inquiring.

Meanwhile the Minnesota clinic continued to urge him to come there, so George reversed his decision and agreed to join its staff. At first I was greatly relieved. But one morning a dark depression settled over me, and I feared that we had made a colossal mistake. Thinking perhaps I had inadvertently applied pressure to my husband, I was oppressed by guilt feelings and

[1] From *My Full Inheritance as a Woman.* Copyright © 1974 by Women's Aglow Fellowship, Lynwood, WA 98036.

walked about the house groaning at the thought that we might be moving outside of the will of God. At last I cried out, "O God, show me somehow whether or not George has chosen the right place!"

As I waited before him, I had a strong desire to get my Bible. I opened to a phrase never before noticed, "Iron is taken out of the earth" (Job 28:2). Now among the sights George had visited in northern Minnesota was the huge iron ore plant and open pit mine in the area, known as the "Iron Range." I had read in the brochures that 60 percent of all the iron in the United States comes from that small area. (Later our post office address was to be Mountain Iron.) The specific nature of that Scripture phrase came to me with the force of revelation. I was not only strengthened—I was endued! The knowledge that we were moving according to his plan gave me hinds' feet on high places for many days. And I was to need that certitude, for my husband's illness in that place made some of our days exceedingly difficult.

For Mary, following hard on the heels of revelation came the strength of joy. She began her own paean of praise, "My soul doth magnify the Lord, and my spirit hath rejoiced in God my Saviour" (Luke 1:46, 47). (Hundreds of years earlier, Nehemiah had also discovered that the joy of the Lord was his strength.) But Mary did more than just stand there and smile while God poured out buckets of blessing from heaven. She strengthened *herself* by voicing praise; *she* magnified the Lord. Her joy was based in part on the realization of her place in history, that she of low estate would be called blessed by all generations. I am always stirred by the scriptural fulfillment of her statement when I hear many Roman Catholic voices reciting, "Blessed art thou and the fruit of thy womb, Jesus."

We, too, may revel in a sense of our divine destiny. "Long ago, even before he made the world, God chose us to be his very own, through what Christ would do for us; he decided then to make us holy in his eyes, without a single fault—we who stand before him covered with his love" (Ephesians 1:4, TLB). I was not only chosen, but monogrammed with the initials of my Creator!

Mary moved quickly, then, into an exalted statement of the

character of God. This understanding of what God is like was a major strength. She was so thoroughly acquainted with Scripture that when Gabriel told her that her son would be given the throne of his father David and that he was to reign over the house of Jacob, Mary recognized the authority of the Holy written Word. In her own song she referred at least seven times to Old Testament Scriptures.

For me, too, the surest way to strengthen myself is to review who God is and what he is like. God himself used this method repeatedly in speaking to his children: "I am the God who brought you out of the land of Egypt," or "I am the God of Abraham, Isaac and Jacob." I may do this by reading his Word and by remembering his mighty acts for me personally. (The Lord tells me that since my memory tends to fade each time I face a new obstacle, I need to keep a journal of his acts of love toward me.) Mary proclaimed that God is mighty, holy, merciful, and strong; she noted that he fills the hungry with good things, that he helps Israel, and that he keeps his word. (See Luke 1:49–55.) Such remembering is the best possible therapy.

Although Mary's praise was public, she herself remained a very private person. Luke tells us twice that she "kept these things," not discussing them with others. There is strength in privacy, in waiting for God's revelations to complete their leavening in us. Sometimes I have shared my spiritual lessons too soon with fellow believers and aborted what the Lord wanted to teach me in time. I am sure God wants us to have some secrets just with him. He will cause us to understand if and when they are to be told. Eventually Mary shared hers with Luke, so that we may be instructed thereby.

Finally, Luke tells us, in Acts 1:14, that Mary experienced the strength of Pentecost. While this is not something she did for herself, she again placed herself where she could receive the promised Comforter. Of the assembled 120, Mary and the twelve are the only ones named. We know many of the transforming results of the Upper Room experience in the lives of the men—those are what Acts is about. But the record doesn't show what followed in Mary's life.

Just now I asked the Lord, "Jesus, how did you strengthen Mary when she was filled with the Holy Ghost?"

"Just as Isaiah prophesied concerning me [61:1]," he answered, "I healed her broken heart."

EIGHT
She Perceives Her Work

She perceiveth that her merchandise is good.
Proverbs 31:18

The virtuous woman is a sampler, a taster, a tester—of her own wares. The verb "perceive" in the Hebrew means "to taste"; it's the same one David used when he wrote, "O taste and see that the Lord is good" (Psalm 34:8).

Earlier we saw the lady weighing and planning shrewdly as she considered a field. Now she is again in the process of examining; and as she evaluates, she perceives. Perception is more than a mental process; it's an intuitive grasp, a "gut-level" knowledge. Intuition is something we women are often credited with—and occasionally blamed for having. God gave it to us, in any case, and there is a time to employ it.

"Merchandise" refers to profit from trade; it has the same root as the "merchants' ships" in verse 14, deriving from a word meaning "to go round." Obviously the Proverbs lady has been busy. But now she takes time to reflect and inspect. (Inspection is usually a good idea. As a young teen mixing a cake, I failed to do that before baking—and I omitted the shortening. My father suggested I contact the War Department which at that early World War Two period was seeking a sturdier synthetic rubber.)

The Proverbs woman's conclusion was that her work was "good." That's the Hebrew word used in the broadest sense for what is pleasing, prosperous, beautiful, pleasant, and gracious.

It's also the same word chosen in the opening verses to declare that she will do her husband only good. (She's still doing him good by producing good merchandise. *Today's English Version* says, "She knows the value of everything she makes.")

To see our work as good is an ability we share with our Father. Five times he looked upon a creative act "and saw that it was good." The sixth time, after he had made man, he looked, and "behold, it was very good." (See Genesis 1:10–31.)

The Israelites had suffered twenty years of severe oppression by the Canaanites when Deborah, the palm tree prophetess and judge, summoned Barak to lead an army into battle against them. Barak, who won for himself a listing in the Hebrews 11 Hall of Fame, promptly replied, "Only if you go with me!"

With equal promptness, Deborah answered, "I will surely go with thee" (Judges 4:9). Since Deborah—and Barak, for she told him, too—already knew how the battle would turn out, I suspect that the reason she was so willing to accompany him was her perception that she had something the army needed to have with them, in this case God's anointing. (I can't speak positively for Deborah, but for *me* to march into an army encampment with 10,000 men for any other reason would, on a scale of 1 to 10, rank no higher than 1½!)

In the victory duet that she sang with Barak, Deborah's opinion of her merchandise is clear: "They ceased in Israel, until that I Deborah arose, that I arose a mother in Israel" (Judges 5:7).

Jan introduced me to this refreshing virtue when we both lived in Fairbanks, Alaska. I had been appointed director of Vacation Bible School, which there and then was an especially important church and community service. Prepared for a hard-sell, I phoned Jan first. "I'd like for you to direct the primary department because you're so well qualified," I began.

But I never got to use the rest of the sales pitch because she quietly replied, "Yes, that's true. And I will do it."

It *was* true, for she was a trained teacher and a skillful and loving manager of her own three toddlers. But I hadn't expected her to admit it, for I'd always observed and participated in the game of demurring and disclaiming our abilities while we enjoyed being coaxed into doing what we planned to do all along. And later every person I recruited in that remarkable church was equally ready. Their merchandise was good and they recognized the fact.

When I read about the ex-cupbearer Nehemiah who became chief contractor for the rebuilding of the Jerusalem walls, I chuckle. His wily enemies, Sanballat and Tobias, tried repeated ruses to halt his project. Finally they attempted the delaying tactic of inviting him to a top-level conference—with them. But Nehemiah, with a grand disregard for humility, sent them word, "I am doing a great work, so that I cannot come down" (Nehemiah 6:3). When they persisted, he repeated his message four times.

Eventually even Nehemiah's enemies and the heathen "perceived that this work was wrought of our God" (Nehemiah 6:16). But their perceiving was the word that means to ascertain by seeing. Anyone can do that. But Nehemiah understood the importance of his work when it was still mostly a pile of rubble.

Like Nehemiah, we also have an enemy who not only tries to destroy our work, but attacks us repeatedly concerning its value. When my first child was nearly five, it seemed time for her to have a dental examination. After carefully discussing it with her, I took her to my dentist, a man I respected and liked. But unaccountably my outgoing, normally obedient child became frightened and behaved badly. My dentist stopped abruptly and said to me sternly, "I refuse to treat an uncooperative person."

Nothing had ever been so stinging as the mortification I felt at that first open disapproval of my child, my "produce." Subsequently I have learned to understand my kids in the light of their own development and God's desires for them, rather than seeing them solely through the eyes of others. But at that time I suffered acutely.

Not long afterward Becky redeemed herself. She had her new dress and hat to wear as a flower girl at the wedding of her beloved Sunday school teacher. But sudden rehearsal fears made her refuse to perform. Dear Rosella, an older woman, was marrying for the first time and we all wanted her wedding to be perfect. Though I offered to let someone else use Becky's dress, Rosella maintained that Becky would be all right, and when she stopped to get her for the wedding, Becky went along.

As the ceremony began, I tried to stay out of sight lest Becky find me a convenient refuge and lose her resolve. My little one went bravely up to the altar. Then she turned, finally spotted me, and gave me a tiny, reassuring wave. So comforted was I, my "work" had value after all.

When David aspired to the position of fighting Goliath, even though the field of applicants was not overcrowded, he did not hesitate to give Saul his credentials. He had, with the Lord's enabling, single-handedly slain a lion and a bear. With those qualifications, he was positive that he and the Lord of hosts would conquer this giant.

Here is an important clue to the reason why we today are entitled to perceive our work and find it good. We are merchandising *for* God—as did Nehemiah and Deborah and Jan and David. The familiar Scripture enjoins us, "And whatsoever ye do, do it heartily, as to the Lord, and not unto men" (Colossians 3:23). That "whatsoever" is a pretty broad term, including attaching collars in a shirt factory, vacuuming the same floors a jillion times, or balancing books in a one-girl office. The Lord has promised that nothing we do for him will go unrewarded.

When Rebecca ran out to water Eliezer's dusty, smelly, cantankerous camels, she performed a very routine task, one which she perceived to be a good and necessary and courteous one. Probably she had not the slightest notion that she was answering a prayer, and that she was about to become the wife of a millionaire, the mother of Israel, and an everlasting type of the beautiful bride of Christ.

We are also working *with* God, as David did when he vanquished his enemies and said, "Through God *we* shall do valiantly" (Psalm 60:12a).

Jesus described an easy yoke, a two-person harness, by which we are joined to him. His very coming was a demonstration of the kind of Helper he is, willing to join us in the often monotonous grime of earth, but beautifying all of its activities with his participation in our lives.

One morning several ladies gathered for a prayer and Bible study time. Most were young housewives, including our hostess of the day whose life just then was especially bitter. In spite of her efforts toward a patient and loving example, her husband continued to be unfaithful, to drink heavily and to be vindictive toward her and their several small children. Each of us, of course, had burdens of some sort.

As we read the Word together and then worshiped with prayer and singing, however, it became an unusually hallowed time.

Then we felt that the Lord Jesus was saying to our hostess, as well as to all of us, "I have brought you out of the miry clay. Now I see your needs and I am with you in every part of your life. Invite me each day into your kitchen and we will have coffee together."

The blessed quietness of that time flooded our hearts with peace and our eyes with healing tears, for we remembered that he had said in Revelation 3:20 that he would come in and sup with those who answered his knock.

Realizing anew that he works and walks with us, as we work and walk with him, made a singular difference in our lives that day, and in the days which followed. Our burdens became light, as he promised, and it was possible to perceive that our merchandise was good.

NINE
Her Candle Lasts

Her candle goeth not out by night.
Proverbs 31:18

Everybody (with the possible exception of light bulb manufacturers), I suppose, loves candles, symbols as they are of romance and mystery and elegance. They aren't noted for their brilliance (which is why Jesus said they needed to be placed on candlesticks), but for their steadfastness. The Proverbs woman had such a candle, or lamp, which was probably an open clay dish containing oil and a wick.

I believe, however, that our heroine not only *possessed* a candle but that she *was* the candle. I read in Proverbs 20:27 that "The spirit of man is the candle of the Lord." Of the wicked Bildad it says, "His candle shall be put out with him" (Job 18:6). But David affirmed to the Lord, "You have turned on my light!" (Psalm 18:28, TLB).

The idea of being a candle delights me.

Especially when I read that I don't have to be extinguished at night!

The durability of the Proverbs lady's candle is linked to her perception of her work. Freely translated, her attitude was something like this: "Because my work is important, I can afford to hang in there."

At the literal level, the words say that she worked late at night. But I think God does not mean merely to extol sleeplessness.

44

The word "night" in the Hebrew also means adversity; thus the *Amplified Bible* says of her candle, "It burns on continually through the night [of trouble, privation or sorrow, warning away fear, doubt and distrust]."

Jochebed lived in the darkness of Egypt when a new king rose who knew not Joseph. But she was determined—and plucky. When she perceived that her offspring was a "goodly child," she first hid him and then displayed him—right in the path of his enemies! (One of the several things I'm tentatively planning for my heavenly agenda is to ascertain from Jochebed how, without acoustical tile, she managed to conceal for even three months a lusty-lunged little male.)

We know the rest of the story. Moses, the infant charmer, sobbed piteously at just the right time to arouse the compassion of a sophisticated princess; and Jochebed, his mother, ended up getting paid for what she wanted most in all the world to do, nurse her own baby boy. She was a lady whose candle refused to be extinguished.

One midmorning Rita and Fred waved goodbye to a couple of their children, Mary, 15, and Susan, 12, as the girls walked a few blocks away to shop. Hours later the girls were declared missing; weeks later their cruelly stabbed bodies were found in an abandoned quarry.

The parents' night was suffocatingly, terrifyingly, grievously dark. Nothing in their quiet, solid, Catholic, middle-class lives portended such an event. These two were shy, careful, "good" girls. Daily Rita had prayed for the protection of their six children.

Sitting with her one afternoon, I heard her cry out, "Did our girls need us at the last and wonder why we could not come?"

Rita thought of the words of Jesus, "My God, why hast thou forsaken me?" At the funeral mass the priest said that these two girls had shared in the suffering and martyrdom of Christ.

Two years later, despite extensive investigations, the murderer(s) had not been found nor any part of the mystery solved. There is not yet any resolution.

But a few months ago when I returned to the area for a visit, this petite lady bicycled across town to meet me in a cafe while my car was being serviced. Rita was always pretty, but I saw that suffering had stamped on her a new beauty. She is often asked, she told me, to tell her story, which involves the sustaining grace and sufficiency of the Lord. Her blue eyes smiled as she told me, "I was the eldest of twelve children and could not be spared from home after the eighth grade. But a few days ago I finally got to high school—and I was *behind* the teacher's desk, speaking to a class about death and dying."

Recently Rita wrote: "Last year I spoke at thirty-five to forty churches and Christian Women's Clubs and have engagements scheduled through November again. It's been a growing and broadening experience for me, and I'm learning how to pace myself, and setting up a businesslike schedule that will not be disruptive to our family life. Fred has encouraged me very much to go out, and so has my pastor, Father Torborg. Every place has had overflow crowds. I'm sure I'm a curiosity because of the nature of my experiences . . . yet I have to believe (I *know*) God has a special message for me to give, and special people to be reached.

"Fred will be ordained as a Permanent Deacon May 31. We can see . . . that his area of ministry will be to the elderly, sick, and dying, and to bereaved families. We are getting more and more involved with bereavement and grief, and ironically we don't find it morbid."

Their candles burn on.

A candle can only keep burning if it has a sufficient supply of oil. Throughout the Word, oil is a type of the Holy Spirit who will, Jesus said, abide with us forever, an undiminishing Source of oil for the candles of our spirits.

How (and when) the Holy Spirit fills our lives and what he does after he arrives (and in what sequence) have frequently and regrettably been matters of dispute among Christians. Though I am not equipped to say the definitive words on the subject, the concept which satisfies me theologically is that, upon my conversion, or my acceptance of Jesus as Savior, the Holy Spirit placed me in Christ: "The Spirit makes you God's sons, and by the

Spirit's power we cry to God, 'Father! my Father'" (Romans 8:15, Today's English Version). (As God's child I am in Christ, for Christ and God are One.)

When I asked for the Spirit's fullness, Jesus placed me in the Holy Spirit. John the Baptist announced, "I baptize you with water but he will baptize you with God's Holy Spirit!" (Mark 1:8, TLB).

Even more simply, I have come to believe that the one fact of overriding importance is that God longs to give the Holy Spirit to those who ask. (See Luke 11:13.)

This beautiful simplicity was not always my privilege. I first heard about being indwelt by the Holy Spirit when I was a child, and I invited his presence. But for various reasons I often doubted that he was still there, so I would ask him in again. Whether or not he had ever left, he was always gracious to reassure me on the basis of my understanding.

As a young mother, after hearing Dr. Lawlor's lucid and moving exposition of the Spirit's rightful place, I sought him once more—and was never to lose that sense of being comraded.

A few years later I learned more about the Holy Spirit and his nature as revealed by the gifts he wants to give God's children. Because this new knowledge seemed to be in conflict with prior teaching, I entered upon a most painful time of searching and sifting. I hadn't yet understood that "God giveth not the Spirit by measure" (John 3:34), and that I could embrace new truth without discarding old. I read many books and articles in a determined intellectual effort. Constantly begging God to show me what was really true, I also read and reread the Acts and the Epistles.

It was not the mental exercise (although I did not regret any of my study), but an attitude of submission, brokenness, and trust, which eventually made me a candidate for every option God had made available for me. And then it was the Holy Spirit himself who directed me to this verse of personal assurance: "Return to your rest, O my soul, for the Lord has dealt bountifully with you" (Psalm 116:7, Amp.).

47

Several lovely things happened as a result of that experience. I loved Jesus more and was surer that he loved me. I became a "Sword swallower," really wanting to read his Word, and I understood it better. Our marriage improved. I started becoming more tolerant and loving. I was able to follow Jude's advice: "But you, beloved, build yourselves up . . . praying in the Holy Spirit" (verse 20, Amp.); and I began to move into what Paul prayed for the Ephesians, "the spirit of wisdom and revelation in the knowledge of him" (Ephesians 1:17).

But one of the happiest developments was my deliverance from a childhood-based terror that I would be left behind at Christ's Second Coming. I had known the fear was there and that it was irrational, but I was powerless to eradicate it. The Holy Spirit, however, did this for me so completely that I was actually able to enjoy our children's discussions and questions about the Rapture. One day as I was preparing them for outdoor Alaska play, they asked, "When Jesus comes, will we have time to put on our boots and parkas and mittens?" And a few months later, after our summer move to Oklahoma, they inquired if there would be air-conditioning on the way!

One of the areas of controversy about the Holy Spirit's empowering concerns an assumed disparity between supernatural manifestations (spiritual gifts) and right living (the fruit of the Spirit). But from a sermon by Pastor Fred of Minneapolis I learned good news. The Lord wants us to have both. To the hem of the high priest's robe were attached alternately a bell and a pomegranate. The pomegranate, of course, is a fruit. The bell symbolizes the sometimes spectacular gifts of the Holy Spirit; in fact, God intended the high priest to be heard when he walked. (We, too, are priests.)

Nor does there need to be a disparity between fun feelings and right behavior. God said through Isaiah that Jesus was coming to give the oil of joy. And the reason for this happy feeling was so that we "may be called oaks of righteousness [lofty, strong and magnificent, distinguished for uprightness, justice and right standing with God], the planting of the Lord, that He may be glorified" (Isaiah 61:3, Amp.).

Wise are the virgins who purchase the oil of the Holy Spirit and find that they have also bought the oil of joy!

The losses of Naomi seem typical of many periods of adversity which God's women have known. Bereft of husband and sons (not only an emotional loss but an economic disaster), her candle directed her back to Bethlehem, where she heard that the Lord was giving his people food. Something in Naomi's light impelled Ruth, a foreign in-law, to accompany her.

Upon their arrival, the disaster of these women seemed so great that the whole town was stirred about them, and Naomi mourned, "I went out full, and the Lord hath brought me home again empty" (Ruth 1:21).

Yet this capable woman taught Ruth how to behave in the grain fields and maneuvered her through the intricacies of persuading Boaz to restore the family fortunes. Though Naomi had no descendants, she lived to cuddle a grandson.

Thus I have found that our process of survival is more than that. We are above the level of those who merely "grin and bear it." The candle which God himself has lighted and which burns on the oil of the Holy Spirit is to us like the gyroscope of a ship or plane, keeping us on course when we may *feel* only the shock of physical injury, the pain of betrayal, or the numbness of grief.

But we don't have to make it happen.

God does.

That's why Jesus could say, "*Let* your light so shine before men." The results, like those for Jochebed and Naomi and my friends Rita and Fred, will be visible. Seeing our good works, men *will* glorify our Father.

TEN
She Opens Her Hands

She layeth her hands to the spindle, and her hands hold the distaff. She stretcheth out her hand to the poor; yea, she reacheth forth her hands to the needy. Proverbs 31:19, 20

One of the most charming vignettes in Scripture is the description of the Shunammite woman planning with her husband to make a guest room. As we listen in on their conversation, we learn that she considers a bed, table, chair, and lamp as essential furnishings. She made these plans, not to gain favors, but to extend generous hospitality to one whom she perceived to be "a holy man of God" (2 Kings 4:9). Elisha, the recipient, appreciated her painstaking and reverent concern.

The Proverbs woman, too, can be described as the lady with the giving hands. Four times in these few words her hands are mentioned. First she made thread and yarn from the wool and flax which she so diligently sought. Her left hand held the spindle and her right the distaff. The word for the right hand refers to its closed position, since she had to grasp the distaff firmly in the spinning process.

She did her spinning at home.

But the products were not limited to her own household. Interestingly, her gifts to others are mentioned before the clothing she made for her family. The "hand" word used in the statement of her outreach, as well as the one with which she held the spindle, signifies the open palm, indicating power, ministry, and service.

50

I wonder how many church sewing circles have taken the name of Dorcas, that fascinating New Testament lady who "filled her days with acts of kindness and charity" (Acts 9:36, New English Bible). Since her name meant gazelle, I think she may have been very beautiful. (Perhaps she was even crowned Miss Joppa of '25!) And apparently she was wealthy.

But Dorcas spent her days, not as a socialite on the party circuit, but in a giving which was personal—she made her garments by hand—and loving, else her death would not have been so devastating. Undoubtedly Christian women were dying fairly regularly, but when Dorcas did, two men disciples hunted up Peter and said, "Hurry!"

What happened next always amuses me. Peter was met in the mortuary room by "*all* the widows" (Acts 9:39) weeping and showing him the tunics and garments Dorcas had made for them. What a predicament for a former fisherman, newly-turned apostle! At a time like that, I suspect he was not remotely interested in the women's clothes sewn by the deceased. No wonder he put them all out of the room before he spoke the words which restored Dorcas alive to the saints and widows.

These three—the Shunammite woman, the Proverbs woman, and Dorcas—gave from positions of financial strength. Blessed are all those who do!

But blessed also are those who give out of their little.

My Aunt Lila was such a one. She and Uncle Lee, a preacher, visited our family the Christmas I was eight and gave me my first Bible. It had a black cardboard cover, and the cheapest paper—but was beautifully red-edged, I thought. The nineteen-cent price, a substantial expenditure out of Uncle Lee's fifteen-dollar-a-month salary, was still visible through the erasure.

My religious education had been sketchy. When I was little, Mother read to me from a Bible story book at night, after which Daddy swung me to his shoulders and chanted, "Shadrach, Meshach, and To-Bed-We-Go," as he carried me to my room. As a preschooler I had gone to a rarely available Sunday school, dutifully memorized "Let us love one another," and thereafter puzzled mightily over the relationship between lettuce and loving.

But now a Bible was mine, and Aunt Lila offered me five cents for memorizing passages she selected. Before they left, I had earned three buffalo nickels for Isaiah 55, the Beatitudes, and Psalm 19. I loved the rhythm of the heavens declaring the glory of God and the firmament showing his handiwork!

Years later Aunt Lila and Uncle Lee invited George (my future husband) to live with them when his parents moved away during his senior year of high school. To him they gave a greatly needed sense of belonging and acceptance. And when Aunt Lila learned that he would have no suit for graduation, she stayed up all night making over two old suits into one so he would have it in time. It was his first suit and the only one he would have until years later when he earned the dress blues of a naval officer.

When this godly woman spent her last weeks in a large and beautiful Phoenix hospital, one of the Sisters remarked, "I come down here every morning just to look at her and get inspiration for my day." Her young physician outspokenly and affectionately expressed his admiration for her keen mind and loving spirit.

Aunt Lila's roommate, a post-surgical patient who belonged in a different section of the hospital, refused to be transferred. "I *have* to stay here," she insisted, "for God is in this room."

In those final earthly days Aunt Lila endured great pain, but out of her weakness she continued to give, with radiance and power.

Liberality has come under attack by modern "experts" in behavioral science. We are told that we may merely desire to put others under obligation to us (which is true) or that we are trying to manipulate people through gifts (which is entirely possible) or that, lacking sufficient self-esteem, we may attempt to gain acceptance for ourselves through gifts (which certainly happens).

But if we attend only to those precautions, we may well end up in as great poverty of spirit as those whose distress should be alleviated.

Once that almost happened to me.

SHE OPENS HER HANDS

Somehow I got the idea that a beloved friend, who I knew was in a financial bind at the time, needed a bright red dress in time for Christmas. With great pleasure I shopped all over town for just the right color and fabric and wrapped it for mailing.

Then I had a dreadful attack of those sober second thoughts mentioned above, plus a few others, and could not make up my mind whether to send it. Having learned, however, that the Lord knows more than the experts, I asked him to show me what I should do.

As I walked around in the kitchen working and praying, my eyes fell on the day's devotional calendar: "Go your way, eat the fat, and drink the sweet, and *send portions* unto them for whom nothing is prepared" (Nehemiah 8:10, italics mine).

Oh, God is good! After that answer, I even enjoyed standing in line at the post office. Several days later I received my friend's letter: "Your package arrived today, and when I pulled out that *beautiful* red material, my husband and I had to stop and marvel in joyful amazement. You see, the director of the Kuhlman choir announced Friday that beginning next month we would begin wearing *bright* solid, one-color dresses instead of the usual white-blouse-black-skirt combinations. It really shook me for a while because I knew I could not afford to get one or even material for one. My own dresses are either pastel or print and the prospect of being eliminated, as you well know, was not pleasant. I thank you and the Holy Spirit."

One would think I'd have learned my lesson. But not long ago I blew it. I felt curiously and strongly prompted to offer Darlene five dollars, but I reasoned my feeling away because she and her husband both worked, I didn't know them very well yet, and they might be offended at the offer. (I wasn't stingy, just shy.) A few days later at our Bible study I "accidentally" overheard Darlene telling some friends how she had prayed for just five dollars to tide them over until payday and God had sent an unexpected refund. Oh my! Not only did I miss a blessing, but I had to ask the Lord and Darlene to forgive my disobedience.

Many of God's people these days are experiencing the special joy of giving to one another in unique ways.

But I'm not sure giving is an option.

I read in 1 Timothy 5:10 that in order to be eligible for church welfare, a widow must have been "well reported of for good works . . . if she have lodged strangers, if she have washed the saints' feet, if she have relieved the afflicted, if she have diligently followed every good work." While I don't plan to become economically dependent upon the church, those words, along with many other scriptural commands, tell me how God feels about giving.

I am grateful for the attention of our schools to the needy. My husband and I visited kindergarten one year during the Thanksgiving season when the children had been bringing canned goods from home. As we walked into the room, one darling, black-haired moppet smiled toothlessly up at us and asked, "Are you the poor?"

But it is clear from the words "needy" and "poor" to whom the Proverbs woman reached out that more than economic want is included. Sometimes money or an object it will buy is not the appropriate thing to give. Thousands of affluent in modern society need time, attention, or love. Wise stewards give to others what they need, although it may not necessarily be what they want. (An active toddler may *want* to play all afternoon, but a smart mother knows he *needs* his nap—and even if he doesn't, she does!)

However limited our resources may seem, there is an encouraging principle found in the words of Peter to the lame man, "Such as I have give I thee" (Acts 3:6). Peter happened to have an expansive understanding of the power in the name of Jesus, and he gave healing. But all of us who are in Christ have something of his fullness to share.

Sometimes our giving may seem like a colossal failure. Don and Olga had come from New York City to teach in Fairbanks when we lived there. Conscious of the Lord's command concerning hospitality, we had them in our home a few times, which they greatly appreciated. It was late one night after they had come to see our new baby boy that Olga joined me in the kitchen to help with dishes and she commented about how good it was to be with us.

I didn't witness much in those days, but I did reply, "That's because of the presence of Jesus in our home."

Immediately Olga looked offended, and she changed the subject. Already very tired, I felt even worse about my blunder.

But after we had left Fairbanks, we heard a strange story. Soon after that, Olga felt an urgency to go to her church and be baptized. A special speaker "happened" to be there at the time and he showed both Olga and Don the way to a deeper and truly committed walk with the Lord. And Olga was telling people that it was the spirit she felt in our home that made her hungry for more of God.

The *Lord* saw to it that my gift did not misfire.

At other times the ones we give to may not even realize they are receiving a gift. While I was taking my children to school one morning, a woman driver ran a stop sign and sideswiped our car. Distraught and upset, she assured me she would pay for the damage, so I took her name and address and hurried on to get the kids to their classes on time. After her first gasp when I told her by phone that the estimates exceeded $200, I never heard from her again. When I called, she was never available, but I did reach her mother-in-law once and she told me the family was on welfare. When I made my accident report to the police, I realized that if we pressed charges or even reported the damage to our own insurance company, we could make things very difficult for that woman.

George and I prayed about our course of action, wanting to know the Lord's plan. George was awakened in the night by a Scripture, "Blessed are the merciful: for they shall obtain mercy" (Matthew 5:7).

I contacted Myrtie, who after talking to the Lord counseled us to make a gift of the $200 in our hearts to this woman. Each time we were tempted to feel reproachful toward her, we were, in the name of Jesus, to freely, gladly grant to her the cost of the damage. Then, Myrtie believed, God would return to us according to his fourfold law of giving: "good measure, pressed down, and shaken together, and running over" (Luke 6:38).

We did. Each time I saw her name and address pinned to our bulletin board, I offered her those dents and scratches, which we never did find the money to have repaired and which substantially reduced the car's worth when we eventually traded it for another.

And God did supply. Just a few weeks later, upon the completion of George's residency, as we prepared to move, the Lord miraculously made it possible for us to purchase a beautiful new home.

In Jesus' name—therein lies the proper method of giving.

Pastor Dave received a phone call from friends concerning a deeply troubled couple who had recently prayed to receive Christ. Pastor followed through, and all of us welcomed those people into the fantastically beautiful fellowship of the St. Cloud Covenant Church.

We put hands and feet to our welcome, though we well knew the prognosis wasn't all that great. Multiple marriages, alcoholism, and jail records were part of the package. Eventually Pastor Dave and his wife Karen took them for a time, chain smoking included, into their own home. Men of the church helped them move. Becky and I provided transportation and laundry facilities. Everyone gave love, especially Karen.

Outwardly at least, our efforts didn't seem to take. They divorced, drinking worsened, and one landed in jail again. But we did not fail, for we had done it as unto the Lord.

Today I read about Mary Magdalene and Joanna and Susanna who out of their own substance were able to minister to Jesus as he walked among them, and I realize how great was their privilege. But I, too, can minister to him out of my substance—to anyone who is poor or needy. He said that whatever I do unto even the least of his brethren I do for him. (See Matthew 25:40.)

Yet once more, hallelujah!

ELEVEN
She Fears Not the Snow

She is not afraid of the snow for her household:
for all her household are clothed with scarlet.
Proverbs 31:21

Our seven years in Alaska brought me to terms with snow. But I have been afraid of other things.

When George announced one evening in Alaska that tent camping was the only kind of vacation we could afford and said, "Let's order our equipment right away," my hands turned cold in the dishwater and fear swept over me.

"We still have two in diapers," I reminded him in dismay.

"They'll survive," he said cheerfully. "We can use disposables. Let's get this pearl-gray tent," he suggested as he researched the catalogs. "It will let in more light on rainy days." I was not reassured.

The equipment arrived. So did departure day. I kissed my washer, dryer, and bathtub a reluctant goodbye—and we were on our way. Hidden Lake was calendar-picture perfect, but it looked terribly deep; and I cautioned the children several times not to get too close.

As soon as the tent was pitched, the children began to squeal and romp inside its newness while a steady stream of maternal remonstrance rent the air: "Becky, keep the kids away from the tent walls! Don't run your truck on the air mattress, Dan! Nora, stop swinging on the leg of the folding table!"

Eventually we zipped them into their brand-new sleeping

57

bags, but they were not sleepy. "Mommy, what day is tomorrow?" Becky asked.

"Sunday," I replied.

"Go to Sunday school and church?" queried baby Nora.

"Oh, no," I explained. "It's too far to drive back."

"I want my own church," said two-year-old Danny soberly.

Brightly I reassured them. "We'll have our own church here among the beautiful trees and birds and lake that God has made."

"Just like at home?" asked Dan.

"Just the same," I glibly promised.

Finally the last giggle stopped and whispers faded away. George turned out the lantern and fell asleep. The doused campfire sputtered fragrantly, accompanying the haunting, three-note descending scale of the golden-crowned sparrow. The summer arctic night was incredibly beautiful and peaceful.

But I lay awake, imagining all sorts of wilderness terrors. The thin tent walls seemed totally vulnerable. Why, a bear, or even a badger—I forced my mind away from such thoughts, prayed, and tried hard to trust the Lord. And at last, despite the narrow hardness of my cot, I slept.

It seemed but a few moments until suddenly I was wide awake. At 4 A.M. the Alaskan summer dawn had already filled our tent with pearl-gray luminescence. I heard stealthy footsteps. My throat went dry. Was it an animal or human intruder? With hammering heart, I rose on one elbow—and looked straight into the guileless blue eyes of my little son. As he stood there in his fuzzy yellow sleepers, a shaft of sunlight from the window flap bathed his blond curls and slumber-kissed cheeks.

Holding out toward me a foam cup just like the ones used for the offering in his junior church at home, Danny softly intoned, "Would you like to give something for Jesus' work?"

Laughter bubbled up inside me as I eased him back to bed.

A few years later we pitched our tent high in Colorado's mountains in what we knew to be bear country; we were settling for the night when George was upset by the discovery that he had forgotten something he considered essential for our protection. Instantly there flashed into mind a Scripture verse I didn't realize I knew, "Some trust in chariots, and some in horses: but we will remember the name of the Lord our God" (Psalm 20:7). As I shared it with my husband, I realized that my own camping fears were completely gone. With his wonderful humor, God had relieved me of them at Hidden Lake.

Our Proverbs lady had prudent fearlessness, a virtue we women need much of today—because there's a lot to be afraid of.

Perhaps we moderns are too fastidious to appreciate fully the character of Jael as described in Judges 4 and 5. Whenever any person rates biblical coverage, I always want to know why; the more that is written the more important I assume the story to be. Jael got eleven verses.

When Barak received his commission from Deborah, he was told that not he but a woman would have the honor of killing Sisera. Noble statesman that he was, he accepted the assignment anyway.

Now Captain Sisera was an unpleasant character, with 900 chariots of iron, who had been harassing the Israelites for twenty years; but there was some sort of peace pact between his king and Heber, Jael's husband. So when the Lord turned the battle against Sisera and he escaped on foot from Barak's troops, he felt safe to accept Jael's invitation to rest in her tent.

That was his first mistake.

Then he drank milk, with its known soporific effects, instead of water. And he fell soundly asleep.

Next comes the exciting part. "Jael Heber's wife took a nail of the tent, and took an hammer in her hand, and went softly unto him, and smote the nail into his temples, and fastened it into the ground: for he was fast asleep and weary. So he died" (Judges 4:21).

That is fearlessness. It's also intelligence, strength, and excellent markswomanship!

Pastor Rosengren told us that there are 365 "Fear Nots" in the Bible because we need one every day of the year. We are even admonished to "Be not afraid of sudden fear" (Proverbs 3:25).

My translation for that verse is "Don't panic when you get scared!" It seems to me that, knowing well the fragility of our feelings, our Heavenly Father is continually saying through the Scriptures and in his daily communion with us, "It's OK, because I'm here."

When we do succumb to fear, he has many kinds of remedies.

Early one morning I had a phone call from a young woman who was part of a prayer and Bible fellowship I was leading. "Virginia," she said, "I have just realized that I am afraid of you. May I come over and talk about it?"

Then *I* was startled! "Lord," I said, "if I've been too obtuse even to know a problem existed, how can I help her with it?"

While I put the coffee pot on, however, the Lord reminded me that *he*, not I, is always the Problem Solver.

As we talked, the Spirit helped my very intelligent friend to clarify a couple of basic problems. One was her childhood terror of her mother's corrosive disposition and harshness in judging her daughter's behavior. The other was a guilty fear that, despite her repeated begging, God had not really forgiven her for past sins.

As she had moved into a closer walk with the Savior, those fears focused into a dread of me. (Was I a mother/authority figure?) How she felt toward me didn't matter a great deal, of course; but it was critically important that the old emotional and spiritual debris be cleared away. To that end, despite the "wiles of the devil," the Holy Spirit gave her courage to face me (it took a lot of that, she later told me). Then the Lord quite literally delivered her.

As we prayed, my friend first specifically asked the Lord for his freedom. While I prayed next, almost without conscious effort, I reached across the table and touched her.

Suddenly she exclaimed, "I'm free! When you touched my shoulder, the heaviness just lifted up and went away! Now I can love you." And she knew that she was forgiven of her sins.

Our Scripture concerning the Proverbs lady does not say, however, that she was not afraid, period. It specifies that she was not afraid of the snow for her household. Considering all that we women face today, that could seem rather minor, especially for those of us in warm climates.

But snow is symbolic of all those kinds of dangers and disasters which we cannot control. By itself, it can be bad enough. During my first year of teaching, I was driving back to my job after the holidays when the swirling flakes so disoriented my lady passenger that she screamed, "Virginia, why are you going backwards?" Right then, I decided we had better stop for the night; we were fortunate to get a room in a home while a hundred others sat out the night in a small restaurant in Fountain, Colorado.

Even as I write, a trucker has just been rescued after being stranded for five days in Ohio's ten-foot snowdrifts.

The word "household" used in this passage is the broadest Hebrew term, implying the extended family or all the persons for whom we have any kind of responsibility. It is my conviction that today's women are spectacularly caring and that their concerns extend far, indeed.

And we are all, I think, more concerned about moral dangers than we are about natural disasters such as fires and floods and earthquakes. But however much we may crusade, we are still limited in what we can do about these moral dangers. They are often like the snow which keeps piling up while we watch helplessly.

No way can I isolate my kids from all the porn, the "filthy communications" they hear daily, the "I'll kill you" threats of the hundreds of other pustules erupting hourly from our infected society.

Oh, but I can *insulate* them! That's what the Proverbs woman did for her family. And that's why she wasn't afraid.

She clothed them in scarlet, *all* of them. Apparently these woolen, crimson garments were woven in two layers so that some say her household was "doubly clothed." I wonder if that's the origin of red flannels? In any case, she could be sure they could be warm. And without central heating, that was important.

We cannot *plan* ahead for whatever snow will fall, but we can *prepare* ahead. Jael did not know that Sisera would pass near her

61

tent. But she had prepared her heart to help her own nation—and she had trained her muscles by driving a lot of tent stakes. Because of her crucial act, the nation of Israel, her extended household, then had rest for forty years.

The word scarlet inevitably reminds us of the harlot Rahab's trust—for herself and all her household—in a piece of red cloth dangling from her window. For many months she had to believe that those two spies she hid *would* get safely back to Joshua, that Joshua's army *would* destroy Jericho, and that the soldiers closest to her part of the wall would *not* be color blind! No wonder Rahab made it into the Hebrews 11 faith list, the only woman besides Sarah to be named there.

The scarlet thread is a beautiful type of the blood of Jesus Christ. It is "nothing but the blood of Jesus" which will escort our families into heaven; and it is nothing but his blood which will keep them "unspotted from the world" until they get there.

It was God who provided the shed blood of his Lamb. But we can introduce our households to him. It's been said that "God has no grandchildren." But the Word indicates that faith is transmittable, for Paul knew that Timothy had the unqualified faith which lived first in his grandmother Lois and then in his mother Eunice. (That's one of the reasons Paul could encourage Timothy not to be afraid—God hadn't given him a spirit of fear but of the "faith of his mothers." See 2 Timothy 1:5–7.)

Happy are those homes where the father, as in Passover days, places the blood upon the lintels and doorposts of his house. But presumably lacking a husband, Lydia in Philippi arranged for the baptism of her household.

My children have a wonderfully wise, godly, and loving father. But I, too, have no greater joy than to share Jesus daily with our "cool" teenagers. Already they recognize sin as the basic social disease. They know that the blood of Jesus provides forgiveness for them when they do sin. They are also very much aware of the benefits with which he daily loads us—such as parking places when we're in a hurry and we ask him.

More than that we cannot do for them when the snow falls.

But that's enough. God the Father, Son, and Holy Spirit will do the rest. For he has promised that he will keep that which we've committed unto him until that day. (See 2 Timothy 1:12.) And that includes our children.

TWELVE
She Dresses Up

She maketh herself coverings of tapestry; her clothing is silk and purple. Proverbs 31:22

Busy as she was for her household, the Proverbs woman also cared for her personal needs. She strengthened herself; she perceived that her work was good. Now we see her giving attention to her furnishings. The Word says she makes them for *herself*; perhaps she had a private boudoir or even separate quarters, as was customary those days in some households.

Various translators refer to these coverings as cushions, rugs, quilts, or carpets. *The Living Bible* says "She also upholsters with finest tapestry." At any rate, it was "soft stuff," appropriate for a semipermanent dwelling such as a tent, and beautiful anywhere. These were pieces that she herself made—all in early Mediterranean.

Unless we live alone, few of us have rooms exclusively ours. But we all share the Proverbs lady's interest in prettying up our surroundings. Thousands today are using or learning skills in weaving, upholstering, and refinishing. I was astonished to learn how little my friend Clara in Duluth originally paid for the old furniture which she had transformed into exquisite antiques.

Corrie ten Boom recounts the joy of receiving a package from home while she was in solitary confinement. It contained, among greatly needed items, a red towel and cookies wrapped in red cellophane. "How Nollie understood the gray color-hunger of prison!"[1] Corrie exclaimed. Inspired, she made a lampshade with the red paper. Then, using the red towel threads, she embroidered on her pajamas bright figures of a curtained window, a flower, and a cat.

God planned that his erstwhile slaves, though still homeless, could feast their eyes on the interior beauty of the wilderness tabernacle. He gave Moses such detailed specifications that they included the color of the embroidery.

For nearly five years, in two homes, we walked on balding, old gold living room floor covering. Several months ago I began praying about replacement, knowing that it would be costly. Recently I just happened to find out about a special buy—for which we had just enough in savings—on new frosty blue carpeting. It has just been installed, and the dingy yellow walls have been painted a light blue; my entire household rejoices in God's good provision.

The desire and ability to make "everything beautiful" (Ecclesiastes 3:11) is something we've inherited from our Father.

The Proverbs woman spent a good deal of energy hunting wool and flax, considering fields, and planting vineyards. She sometimes toiled late at night and worked hard at spinning and weaving. But when she came home to relax, those cushions and rugs provided comfort.

I am grateful that the Lord is interested in our comfort, too. More, that he speaks comfortably to us and is himself my Refuge, and my Comforter.

The Proverbs woman was also attentive to her personal apparel.

As Miss Mississippi several years ago, my friend Scotty advanced to the Miss America pageant. Thereafter she forsook music and opted for nursing so that she could better help people. But disease mauled her lovely body until at thirty-nine she was dying from a rheumatic heart, an irreversibly damaged liver, lung disease, and kidney malfunction.

[1] From *The Hiding Place*. Copyright © 1971 by Corrie ten Boom and John and Elizabeth Sherrill. Published by Chosen Books, Inc. Used by permission.

Preparing for death, but not afraid of it, she began to read her Bible and to sense God powerfully. Then at 5 P.M. on a November 22, a miracle happened: "I had just stepped out of the shower," she said, "when suddenly I was instantly made whole—whole from head to toes, exactly as if I were twenty years old and had been given a brand new body."

The first week after her healing, Scotty, who had been unable to sweep the kitchen floor without taking nitroglycerin, celebrated by painting their garage. She ran everywhere. And everywhere and to everyone, with a radiant, happy, healthy countenance she said, "Jesus has healed me!"

As she sought fellowship with God's people, some of them exhorted her: "Now you must let your hair grow (but do it up tightly), leave off all your makeup, and wear everything longer."

Willing to please the Lord she now loved with her whole being, Scotty, who had always dressed and behaved modestly, complied. And she promptly lost her joy. Soon she realized that the drabness of her appearance was ruining her testimony. Although the gift of instant sleep had been part of God's healing package, one night she was wakefully troubled about her new image. At 2 A.M. she stole out of bed to the bathroom sanctuary where Jesus had healed her and cried out to God for his answer.

"Immediately," she said, "God showed me the second chapter of Colossians, for I wouldn't have had any idea then where to read: 'Let no man therefore judge you. . . . Let no man beguile you of your reward in a voluntary humility. . . . Why . . . are ye subject to ordinances . . . after the commandments and doctrines of men?' At once I had my answer. I was to live according to the commandments of God and not the rules of men; I was at peace. From then on, I simply tried to please God and did not worry about what people thought.

"After that," Scotty continued, "God often provided beautiful clothing for me. Once he stopped me with a flat tire in front of a dress shop where I found a lovely, expensive dress marked down to ten percent of its original price. God never 'dressed me down.' He dressed me up!"

The Lord treats each of his children uniquely, of course.

Another friend, as she listened carefully to her Lord, was instructed to eliminate from her grooming a specific item which for her had become a matter of pride.

But I cannot imagine where the notion ever originated that a God who made lions, swans, and impalas; roses, peonies, and jonquils; or cardinals, orioles, and peacocks ever planned for his children to live in graceless, navy-black-and-brownness.

God tells us that the clothing of the Proverbs woman was of "linen, pure white and fine, and of purple" (Proverbs 31:22, Amp.).

The "silk" of the King James version refers to an especially fine quality of linen which grew only in Egypt and had to be imported from there. (That's undoubtedly why she had to seek it.) This is another of God's exciting insights, for he tells us in Revelation 19:8 that "fine linen is the righteousness of saints." We may wear cotton-polyester outside, but inside we can be garbed in the holiness of the perfect One who was made sin for us that we might be made righteous in him.

Hagar, Sarah's maid, had no choice when she was given to Abraham to bear him an heir. But then, realizing that she had conceived by one of the richest, most powerful men in the country, she got uppity. And when Sarah punished her, Hagar, whose name means "Flight," ran away into the wilderness.

So far, it's not a very pretty story.

But it gets better. The angel of the Lord found her, called her by name, and encouraged her to pour out her story. Then he promised this Egyptian girl, whose culture made fertility so very important, that she would have a son who would become a great nation.

It's incredible, but this fugitive slave girl with a bad attitude, unmarried and pregnant with a child who was not part of God's plan, became the first person in recorded history to see an angel and the first to have her child Ishmael named, before birth, by Jehovah. It is not surprising that she worshiped, then, in astonished reverence, "Thou God seest me."

God may not be able to look upon sin, but he could "see" Hagar because she was part of the household of Abraham (as are we in Christ) whose faith was counted unto him for righteousness.

All of us who believe on Jesus were winners when we drew our lot for the seamless robe of Christ's holiness. Lots of days it seems as if every few minutes I need to wrap a little tighter in the fine linen which is, in Christ, the righteousness of the saints.

The Proverbs woman's clothing, adds the *Amplified Bible*, was "such as that of which the clothing of the priests and the hallowed cloths of the temple are made."

This inspires me.

God gave Moses careful details for the habiliments of the priests. They were to wear fine linen robes and purple—the ephod and a curious girdle.

The work of the priests was also well defined. Chiefly they were to minister praises to the Lord, bless the people, and offer sacrifices to make atonement and intercession for the people.

I believe it is our privilege as New Testament women, who are part of what Peter refers to as a "holy" and "royal" priesthood, to perform these priestly functions, "to offer up spiritual sacrifices," and "to shew forth the praises of him who hath called you out of darkness into marvellous light" (1 Peter 2:5, 9).

Miriam the prophetess, even before God instituted the priesthood, became a praiser. Pharoah and his army had just been swallowed up in the Red Sea, so Moses and the men became a choir, singing nineteen verses "unto the Lord. " But they must have needed sopranos and altos to complete the harmony, for Miriam and all the women danced and sang with timbrels: "Sing ye to the Lord, for he hath triumphed gloriously; the horse and his rider hath he thrown into the sea" (Exodus 15:21).

If God made a videotape, when I reach heaven I want to see the singing, swaying magnificence of hundreds of thousands of men and women, who have just watched the annihilation of their cruel oppressors, lift their voices in mighty antiphonal praise to their Deliverer. Or will we be treated to a live performance as was John (Revelation 15:3) who recorded that "they sing the song of Moses . . . and the song of the Lamb"?

As we practice praising, it becomes more and more a natural

expression. A few weeks ago I loaded my groceries into the car—and left my purse behind in the shopping cart in the parking lot. As soon as I reached home, I realized my mistake and hurried back, praying out loud very earnestly as I drove, and trying very hard to praise the Lord, too. My heart sank as I reached the lot and saw only empty carts.

But as I got out of the car, I saw a lovely, gray-haired lady (in a beautiful red dress!) coming toward me. "Are you Mrs. Leih?" she asked.

"Oh," I said, "do you have my purse?"

"Locked right here in my car," she answered. "I had just tried to phone you." (The Lord preserveth the simple.)

Fervently I exclaimed, "Praise the Lord!"

With equal fervor, she responded, "Amen!"

We are discovering today not only the privilege of praise but the benefits of blessing.

When Ruth and Boaz had their baby boy, the neighbor women came by to congratulate Naomi. After they had blessed the Lord, they blessed her: "And may he be to you a restorer of life, and a nourisher and support of your old age, for your daughter-in-law who loves you, who is better to you than seven sons, has borne him" (Ruth 4:15, Amp.). Then these women even named the baby—Obed, which means "Serving."

Blessings, I believe, are even more effective than curses—and lots more fun. To say to another, whether audibly or inaudibly, "I bless you in the name of the Lord," can help God give him his daily load of benefits (Psalm 68:19). To give a specific blessing, as did Naomi's friends, can be a delightfully creative spiritual exercise.

I haven't seen one friend for a couple of years. But recently I answered my phone, and over the hum of long distance I heard, "Grace and peace to you through our Lord Jesus Christ!" And I knew it was Jean. Still a new Christian, she skillfully blesses.

We may also participate in the intercessory ministry of the priesthood. But it is not easy to wear the purple garment of an intercessor. When Jesus wept over Jerusalem, he demonstrated the agony of interceding. It's understandable that many Christians over the years have spoken of it as "carrying a burden."

Rizpah was an intercessor; and though hers is a grisly story, it is worth noting. Her two sons were among seven whom David, following the Lord's instructions for justice, allowed the Gibeonites to kill. But those warriors left their victims' bodies hanging, a needless insult. Rizpah, then, "spread sackcloth upon a rock and stayed there through the entire harvest season to prevent the vultures from tearing at their bodies during the day and the wild animals from eating them at night. When David learned what she had done, he arranged for the men's bones to be buried" (2 Samuel 21:10–12, TLB).

I am touched when I think on the tenacity and single-mindedness of that bereaved mother's vigil.

Just as the priests carried their sacrifices to the altar and left them to be burned, and Rizpah's marathon came to an end, so I have had to learn not to carry my intercession indefinitely. God will give a release (some call it "praying through") and we are to accept it. Frequently I have to relearn this principle; I also have to learn to bear no burdens which God does not want me to carry. Not all concerns are mine.

But it is an exalted privilege to intercede. When I first walked into the home of a new friend, I thought, *This must be a woman who prays.* Later as we would pray in her home, I sometimes felt so surrounded by God's presence that I could almost hear the rustle of angel wings. She *is* a woman of constant intercession, although a very busy one—and a happy one. Two of her favorite words to describe God's answers are "fun" and "exciting." And I made sure she knew about this book because I needed her prayers as I prayed and wrote.

Intercession can be a calling. Another of my single friends looks toward the time when she can support herself by part-time work and spend eight hours a day in intercessory prayer.

Our intercessory purple may well be the most critically important color we ever wear. In the aftermath of Korah's rebellion against Moses, the entire complaining congregation was in mortal danger. God said to Moses, "Get out of the way so that I may consume these people."

Instead, Moses sent Aaron, the priest and intercessor, into the midst of the people with a censer containing fire from off the altar. "Aaron did as Moses had told him to, and ran among the people, for the plague had indeed already begun; and he put on the incense and made atonement for them. And he stood between the living and the dead, and the plague was stopped" (Numbers 16:47, 48, TLB).

God said, "I sought for a man . . . that should . . . stand in the gap" (Ezekiel 22:30). Likewise the intercessory prayers of just one of us can mean the difference between life and death.

My friend Joan in Alaska was once impressed to pray earnestly for Ray, a missionary pilot. Later she learned that at that very hour he was in a perilous flying situation through which the Lord guided him safely.

When my son was a sixth grader, his class took an all-day trip to a conservation camp in the Minnesota woods. Along with other parents, I had seen a slide presentation of the program, which indicated nothing more hazardous than wet feet; and anyway, I'm not usually a nervous mamma. But at 12:45 the Holy Spirit broke into my thoughts with a sharp command: "Dan is in danger; pray for him." I obeyed and then had peace about him.

The next day Dan told me, with disgust. "Mom, do you know they had us practicing Transcendental Meditation at that camp?"

"Was it just after lunch?" I asked.

"Yes," he said. "They wanted us to rest, so one of the leaders told us to let our minds go blank and then think of one word."

"What did you do?"

"I just kept talking to my friends," Dan replied.

Then I told him how the Lord had prompted me to pray for him, and we talked about the fact that God had prepared us a few days earlier by allowing us to hear an excellent radio interview with a knowledgeable young man who explained why TM is not Christian. "But if it ever happens again," I said to Dan, "just keep thinking of Jesus."

Perhaps someday on the heavenly computer we may learn for

the first time of occasions when as intercessors we have stood between the living and the dead.

Romans 8:28, that lifeline promise which says that everything works together for good to us who love the Lord and are called according to his purpose, is preceded by a discourse on intercessory prayer. Some feel that is the purpose for which we are called. The encouraging part is not only that the Holy Spirit will tell us what to pray for, but that he joins in the prayer according to the will of God, *which he always knows!*

We can't be losers, when we're intercessors. Or praisers or blessers.

I find in Scripture that fine linen and purple were also used by royalty. The palace wall hangings of King Ahasuerus were fastened with fine linen and purple (Esther 1:6); and when, after the demise of the wicked Haman, Mordecai was made prime minister, he "went out from the presence of the king in royal apparel ... with a garment of fine linen and purple" (Esther 8:15).

We, too, are of royal lineage. As King's daughters, we are "all glorious within" (Psalm 45:13). And Jesus Christ who "loved us and washed us from our sins in his own blood" also has made us kings and priests. (See Revelation 1:5, 6.)

Thank you, Lord Jesus for giving me priestly, regal clothing to match what you've said you made me to be.

THIRTEEN
She Promotes Her Husband

Her husband is known in the gates, when he
sitteth among the elders of the land.
Proverbs 31:23

The description of the ideal woman started with her husband and his trust in her. Now he shows up again, this time having profited from a wife who has devoted herself to doing him good all the days of her life.

He "sits in the gates," suggesting the function of making important decisions or judgments. He is a city councilman or perhaps a senator. The bargaining of Boaz when he redeemed Ruth's inheritance and the right to marry her, with the elders witnessing the transaction at the gates of the city, illustrates the position of Mr. Proverbs.

A footnote in the *New Berkeley Version* says, "His wife has aided him toward his success." How did she do this? Did she entertain his boss, or make campaign speeches, or send periodic news releases of his accomplishments to local couriers? Or did she simply go about the affairs of her household with such competence that he was free to become a responsible and respected leader?

I find great pleasure in being with a woman who promotes her husband. Juanita does this beautifully. Many years ago when we first met her and her husband Bill, she was by far the most enthusiastic fan in his cheering section. It wasn't that she carried signs, or boasted of him constantly, or even that she pushed him—rather that her whole manner demonstrated her respect for and joy in him. (It was mutual.) Even when Bill was forced to change his career plans, her loving faith in him was unshaken.

Beginning as a missionary teacher, Bill has steadily risen these twenty years, carefully treading the mazes of cultural and African nationalistic pitfalls, to a directorship. Both on his station and in government circles he sits among the elders of the land. Today he is seeing some of his first students themselves assume positions of honor and responsibility. And Juanita has recently been relieved of her strenuous nursing duties to serve as full-time director's wife and station hostess.

After God spoke to Jacob in a dream, commanding him to leave Laban's employ, Jacob called his two wives to him in the field. He courteously explained to them the deterioration in his relationship with their father and relayed God's orders to depart.

Although up to that time a desperate rivalry had characterized the married lives of these sisters, at that point they were beautifully united in purpose with each other and with their husband. "Rachel and Leah answered him, 'We no longer have any part or lot in our father's house. Does he not look on us as foreigners, now that he has sold us and spent on himself the whole of the money paid for us? But all the wealth which God has saved from our father's clutches is ours and our children's. Now do everything that God has said'" (Genesis 31:14–16, NEB).

Happy is that husband whose wife encourages him to obey God!

In contrast, Michal, daughter of Saul, looked out of her window and saw David dancing before the Lord as he returned from successfully bringing home to Israel the ark of the Lord. With bitter sarcasm, she denounced what she considered his unroyal behavior. As a result, she "had no child to the day of her death" (2 Samuel 6:23, Amp.). Perhaps a clue to her behavior is that only once is she called David's wife, while ten times in Scripture she is identified as Saul's daughter.

Happy is the woman who truly leaves her father's house.

My mother and we girls were at our annual family reunion and apple-canning time on my aunt's Iowa farm when a cataclysmic letter came from my daddy back in South Dakota. Though he'd only been a Christian a little while, he was already a man of much prayer. As he was praying and plowing, he felt the Lord's presence in an unusual and powerful way, he wrote, so he stopped the tractor and got on his knees in the field, telling God that all he was and had belonged to him. He realized, then, that God was calling him to preach.

"I don't see how God can use an ignorant old cow-puncher like me," Daddy concluded his letter, "but if he can, I'm his. Do you think you can manage to help me through the years of preparation and then be a preacher's wife?" (My father was *not* ignorant. But he'd finished only the eighth grade, and he was nearly forty; few adults in those days had money or opportunity to go back to school.)

As for the question he addressed to Mother, I'm sure he knew the answer before he asked. She cried for joy when she read his letter aloud to the assembled family. (Aunt Lila and Uncle Lee wiped their eyes and praised the Lord.) She well knew that with three young children, the smallest just a baby, the road would not be easy.

And it wasn't. After Daddy sold everything at a farm auction and moved to Nampa, Idaho, to take the Bible Certificate course at NNC, there were many "trials of faith." The baby broke her arm. The battery was stolen from our car, and my bicycle from school. He lost some of the dairy cows he bought for our livelihood, and the best ones perversely did not bear female calves which would have been worth far more money. (This situation once prompted my youngest sister, when her turn came at family devotions, to beg fervently, "And dear God, *bless* Spot's calf, even if he is a bull!")

Our house burned down, and Mother lost her engagement and wedding rings along with most of our necessities.

My father, who had ridden a handsome bay over thousands of acres of open range and then managed the complexities of dirt farming, had to tuck his half-soled shoes under a thirty-inch desk and accept assignments. His first semester's grades, although respectable, weren't what he'd have liked, and from our basement I overheard him tell Mother that he was just a dumb farmer after all and he'd better quit trying to become a preacher.

Mother has a meek and quiet spirit, but that time she rose up in her inner woman and emphatically declared, "Leo, God called you to preach and he will see you through. We did not come this far for you to quit! I'll learn to milk the cows and get a job so you can have more study time."

And she did. Overcoming my father's Irish chivalry which had always before kept her out of the barn, she took over many of the dairy chores. And this woman, who had a college degree qualifying her to teach, went to work in a potato and onion dehydrating factory—on the graveyard shift so she would be home daytimes with the youngest. She even took in sewing. And my father's scholarship became such that the college president offered him the opportunity (which he declined) of remaining longer in school and earning a degree.

We ate a lot of macaroni, and our wardrobes were so limited that when Spot's calf ate part of the laundry hanging on the line, it was a real catastrophe. When my father finished school and my parents were moving to his first pastorate, I tried to help Mother carry up from the basement the cardboard-reinforced mattress which my parents had used during those years. Every time we got a firm grasp, the flimsy innards came loose in our hands; finally we collapsed on the steps in helpless laughter. But at no time did I ever hear Mother complain, nor did I detect in her anything but pride in Daddy and his calling.

Not long ago we three sisters planned a golden wedding anniversary celebration for our parents. Although I knew they were highly esteemed, I was surprised at the great love and respect expressed by the many who came—businessmen, executives, educators, and dozens of beautiful "ordinary" people. Their lives had been strengthened and sometimes eternally transformed by their association with a man who obeyed God and a woman who aided him with every ounce of loyal energy she possessed.

76

I realize there are women with husbands whose activities they cannot wish to advance. I believe that if mine were a bartender or land fraud promoter or a mafia-type hatchetman, I could not support his work. But I could seek to promote him personally so that he would feel so good about himself he wouldn't need to be dishonest.

Thousands of women do not have husbands. For them, and even in a larger sense for those of us who do, I believe God also has a lesson—and a promise. We are to glorify and magnify the Lord.

The first phrase to burst from the lips of the Virgin Mary when she received God's promise was "My soul doth magnify the Lord!"

One Sabbath while teaching in a synagogue, Jesus saw a woman bent double by a demon of infirmity. Calling her to him, he released her from this bondage.

Instantly this woman, who for eighteen years had been able to see nothing but bugs and dirt and lizards, stood upright. Now she could see clouds billowing in Israel's deep blue skies, the olive trees shining in the sun, and beauty and compassion in the face of Jesus. Her first act was to glorify God. (See Luke 13:13.)

But magnifying the Lord is not exclusively a verbal exercise. Literally, it means that others will see in us, as through a magnifying glass, Jesus Christ.

That's a tall order for finite me.

It's also a philosophy and a way of life which is completely contrary to the life-style which our society currently advocates for women, to say nothing of going against the grain of our natural inclinations. The little girl in me constantly clamors, "Notice me," and I must constantly respond, "Not I, but Christ."

I find in Scripture a number of ways in which I may glorify or magnify the Lord without necessarily saying anything. I can, like Abraham, believe the promises of God (Romans 4:20). The spirit of glory also rests upon me when I suffer for the Lord (1 Peter 4:14)—even when I don't feel as if I'm glorifying the Lord at such a time, it's true because God said so.

A third method is described in part of Paul's prayer for the

Philippian Christians: "May you always be doing those good, kind things which show that you are a child of God, for this will bring much praise and glory to the Lord" (Philippians 1:11, TLB).

Then there is the all-encompassing statement in 2 Thessalonians 1:12, "That the name of the Lord Jesus Christ may be glorified in you." Paul adds, "and ye in him." I love the mutuality of this—the togetherness of Jesus and me.

Togetherness with fellow believers helps, too, David found, for he sang, "O magnify the Lord with me, and let us exalt his name together" (Psalm 34:3).

In a letter to us written early in his pastoral ministry, my father expressed his aspirations: "I want to be just the kind of salt lick where the flock can come and be made thirsty for the water of life."

Sometimes I must consciously correct my stance in this matter. Recently I bought a new dryer with the stipulation that it be delivered the following day. Although I waited all day, it didn't come. The store phoned an apology and gave a firm commitment for the next morning. Again I stayed home, and again it did not arrive—and I had, besides errands, a load of damp clothes going stale in the washer. Another phone call brought the assurance of its arrival that afternoon. It was after five when it finally came, and I greeted the delivery man with something less than cordiality.

Then *he* was cross! And I began receiving all kinds of uncomfortable signals from the Holy Spirit concerning my failure to glorify my Lord. So I apologized, and the young man apologized (someone had sent him in the opposite direction that day and he was feeling even more frustrated than I). The Lord told me very emphatically that he hadn't placed me here so that my plans and schedules would always mesh; rather his intention was that I should represent him with patience and courtesy. (He did say there are occasions when we must be firm stewards of the time and money he gives us, but that hadn't been one of them.)

Most of the time, however, I believe we simply "abide in the vine" and the fruit which results will bring honor to the Vine-dresser.

Sometimes that happens when we least expect it. My sister Pat recently took a summer course in Denver during an unprecedented heat wave. Her un-air-conditioned upper dorm room faced west into the afternoon sun. A profuse perspirer, she is more uncomfortable in hot weather than any person I know. Showering in the steamy, communal bathroom didn't do a lot to alleviate her discomfort.

But in that bathroom she frequently met another student, a small, neat, quiet-voiced older woman. Over hand laundry or tooth brushing, they exchanged unimportant comments about things like weather and class schedules. Pat learned that the woman was a retired teacher who had saved enough to take a long-wished-for writers' course. But in no way were those humid encounters designed to bring out the best of my sister's disposition or talents.

The morning the woman was to leave, she suddenly said to Pat, in the bathroom where every one of their conversations took place: "You know, you have the sweetest face. You have such a glow that last night I wrote a poem about you, and I think my instructor will like it."

"I was so startled," Pat said, "that all I could do was stammer 'Thank you.' To my knowledge, *nobody* has ever before written a poem about me. I didn't have the presence of mind to ask to see it or even, regrettably, to learn the lady's name."

The best Bible example I know of magnifying the Lord is the donkey who carried Jesus into Jerusalem on Palm Sunday. This little beast (1) received no praise for himself, (2) uttered no words, (3) carried his load without complaining, (4) had no concern about his own worthiness, (5) went exactly where he was led, (6) had the presence of Jesus and (7) bore a triumphant Christ!

Lord Jesus, let me be *your* donkey.

FOURTEEN
Her Influence Spreads

She maketh fine linen, and selleth it; and
delivereth girdles unto the merchant.
Proverbs 31:24

The Proverbs woman has clothed her household and then herself; now she moves into the marketplace with her products.

This is the third mention of flax, the processing of which was no small task. After the harvest, bundles of flax were soaked in water. Then the flax was cut and dried and beaten out. (Rahab hid the two Israeli spies under flax drying on her roof, remember?) Then it was carded by being drawn through the teeth of wooden or metal combs placed on inclined planks. Finally the strands were ready to be spun and woven into cloth. The Proverbs woman's search has resulted in a supply sufficient for her to sell to others the fine linen she has made.

She also delivered girdles to the merchants, who were likely the renowned Phoenician traders of the East. Some of these girdles were made of very rich and precious materials and sold to the wealthy to be used by both men and women. Others were leather garments, like wide belts, used to support the middle back when their wearers were at work. They were often the only garments which had pockets for tools or coins, as most clothing was constructed without so much as a collar, cuff, or pocket. Thus the girdle is often used in the Bible as a symbol of service. The word "delivereth" includes not only distribution but also manufacture; it is likely that the Proverbs woman made the girdles she delivered.

Her resources are such that she has now become a businesswoman, and an independent one at that. Hers was a home-based industry, as were nearly all businesses in those times.

But the desire for profit was not the only consideration for ancient merchants; sometimes there was also a willingness to share goods with those who needed them—as in the case of the Egyptians' storing corn under Joseph so they would have enough to sell during the coming famine.

The Proverbs woman reasoned: "A need exists for fine linen and girdles. I can produce them and profit thereby, so I will proceed."

I suppose that more women are in the business world by choice today than ever before. I was there teaching for several years and am there, in a sense, again with these words I am writing.

Recently the top leader at a denominational conference was quoted in the national press as blaming working mothers for the present shaky condition of the family. Unequivocally he declared that mothers should stay home.

Feminists, on the other hand, have infiltrated all secular and some religious media with the persistent and insidious suggestion that the woman cannot truly be "herself" unless she is in the marketplace. My son had a classmate whose mother felt the need to discover herself, so she abandoned a husband who loved her and two beautiful children. Some are now moderating their stance to concede that "if having babies is your 'thing,' you have a right to do that."

Personally, I regard the religious leader's statement as too sweeping and simplistic. All mothers cannot stay home. And some of them probably shouldn't. On the other hand, there is a basic flaw in hard-line feminist reasoning for those of us who are committed Christians. Our first priority is not to be "ourselves," or even to do our "thing," but to follow Christ's pattern for our lives. That plan will always be uniquely suited to us and totally and joyously rewarding. It may, of course, take a while for us to discover what it is and follow it closely.

We are told about two New Testament women who were in business; both found Paul and Jesus Christ as a result. Lydia, the seller of purple, was a gregarious merchant who undoubtedly influenced many besides her own household to become believers. And Priscilla, with her husband Aquila, was a tentmaker whose occupation is mentioned even before her ministry is noted. In Romans 16:3 Paul says that this couple were not only his helpers but that they risked their lives for him. Did their knowledge of the business world particularly qualify them for this exciting cloak-and-dagger work? That's another story I want to hear in heaven!

Other Bible women assumed public positions which today we would call professions. Women as well as men were singers in the temple choirs. Miriam, Huldah, Anna, and Deacon Philip's four daughters were prophetesses. Deborah was both prophetess and judge. There was also a "host of women who publish" (See Psalm 68:11, Amp.).

For Esther, being queen approached the status of a profession. Not only did she spend a year preparing for her tryouts (and was voted Miss Congeniality in the process, according to Esther 2:15), but after she was crowned, she conducted her campaign for her people with all the finesse of a professional.

I have always enjoyed reading about the daring request of the five daughters of Zelophehad: Mahlah, Noah, Hoglah, Milcah, and Tirzah. Their father had no sons, but they saw no reason why they themselves should not have an inheritance in the Promised Land; so they went before Moses to ask.

Moses was smart enough to realize that he didn't know the answer, so he "brought their case before the Lord" (Numbers 27:5, Amp.).

The Lord replied that the ladies were right and their request should be granted. (Besides their courage, I admire the faith of these five; for the Jordan had not yet been crossed nor one square yard of Canaan possessed!)

Taking no chances, these sisters presented themselves again

before Joshua, reminding him of the agreement they had reached with Moses; and he gave them a portion of the land. Since the names of the middle three mean Flattery, Magpie, and Counsel, I choose to classify these intrepid women as lawyers!

Later we are specifically told that the Proverbs woman did not neglect her household, even though she ran a business. I am sure this is an important principle to help mothers—and other women—decide whether or not they should enter the marketplace.

I am grieved when I hear young women employees in shops and stores say something like this: "I tried staying home, but by the time the baby was six weeks old, I was ready to climb the walls; so I came back to work."

I well know that when one has actively associated with adults in the business or professional world it is very difficult to adjust to being suddenly confined with a small person who is not very intellectually stimulating—but very demanding. Yet I also know that if we give the Lord time, he will help us develop our own resources and will also bring to us the external challenges we need, and we will find child-raising and homemaking the most exciting and creative opportunity available to us.

Abundant literature tells us of the crucial importance of loving child care in the early years. At a medical lecture a few years ago my husband heard a European psychiatrist suggest that one of the reasons for the abominable way in which Americans treat their elderly is that the parents have not cared for their children properly. He further felt that Americans tend to push their adolescents out of the nest too soon. "If you nourish your children properly when they're young," he averred, "they will take care of you when you're old." I believe his point is worth considering.

Even a woman whose children are grown needs to ponder carefully the matter of employment. One of my friends once remarked, "I think it's almost a sin for a Christian woman to go to work *only* because she's bored. There are lonely shut-ins and the ill to be visited, and many more child evangelism classes which could be formed if teachers were available."

One of my acquaintances, though a childless woman, felt that God was calling her out of the classroom where she had happily taught for several years, and was about to be promoted to a principalship, at a time when her husband's new business was still shaky.

"The first year I stayed home and prayed for my husband," she told me, "he made more money than the two of us ever had. And I had time for the many things I'd always wanted to do for the Lord."

Later it appeared as though God was leading her back into a business where she would not only be able to do his work but also utilize her considerable talents and skills.

The working Christian, however, can be greatly blessed. As a teenager waitressing one summer, I enjoyed serving an unusually attractive and considerate young family. After I observed them ask a table blessing I identified myself to them as a believer. When I cleared their table, I found my tip wrapped in a notebook page upon which the man had written, "The Lord make you in every place to manifest the savor of his knowledge." That young man's prayer for me, based on 2 Corinthians 2:14, left me with a lasting glow.

The woman who works by God's design can also have a powerful impact. Several months ago I became aware of this as never before. I was in the hospital for major surgery and already in the cold surgical theater, strapped, stripped, and IV'ed—when there came an unaccountable delay. For an hour and a half the surgeon failed to arrive. My sedation wore off, I became greatly chilled, and fear fought to gain entrance through my spiritual barricades.

Then I heard my surgical nurse humming through her mask, "Joy Is Like the Rain," a song by the Medical Missions Sisters which I especially enjoy. As we talked about sacred music and she sang snatches of new songs she'd heard, the long moments were shortened and I was strengthened; I thanked God for arranging that she should be with me then.

The operation was more complicated and the recovery longer than anyone expected. But God sent another of his choice servants to me, Becky who worked a few evenings a week. While she was preparing me for surgery, she said about the Bible on my table, "I appreciate that." Afterward, when my discomfort was acute, I was surprised to realize that her presence in my room brought instant relief. In my physical weakness it seemed I had a heightened awareness of the spiritual power emanating from one of God's children.

Since then, Becky has told me that she works only as much as the Lord directs and as she feels will not adversely affect her family. And she regards her employment not only in terms of dollars but as a service to her Master. I knew then why God especially anointed her work.

My friend and former student, Margie, is a bundle of effervescence who likes children and good times. Combining these enjoyments, she and a friend went into business catering kids' parties—complete with balloons, games, and food. She quite literally "has a ball." Then, still with time to spare from her homemaking, she formed a professional house-cleaning agency. A few years ago the family needed extra income for a trip, so she took some of the weekly jobs herself.

Immediately Margie found herself witnessing and often leading to the Lord the rich or bored or lonely women whose houses she cleaned. Sometimes she took them to Christian Women's Club luncheons, experiences new to them, which they drank in thirstily; she watched some of her employers blossom into dedicated and fulfilled believers.

"Now we don't need the money," Margie told me, "but every time I ask the Lord if he wants me to quit, he sends me another job—and another person with a deep need."

This attitude—basing our decision on the wishes of our heavenly employer—will make home a haven or business a pleasure.

Whatever we do according to the will of God will be righteous, and he has promised that "the work of righteousness shall be peace; and the effect of righteousness, quietness and assurance for ever" (Isaiah 32:17).

FIFTEEN
She Is Secure

Strength and honour are her clothing; and she shall rejoice in time to come. Proverbs 31:25

Sarah was a magnificent woman. God went to a great deal of trouble, sometimes rearranging the lives of kings, to insure that only she and only Abraham would be the parents of the seed he promised Abraham. Then the Holy Spirit carefully recorded these details so we would know this was so.

Sarah's story begins in Genesis 11:29 and does not conclude until Genesis 24:67. She is mentioned sixty-one times in Scripture, three of those in the New Testament. One entire chapter is devoted to her death and burial; she is the only woman in the Bible whose age at death, 127, is given. God said that the death of his saints is precious in his sight (Psalm 116:15), so we know how he regarded Sarah.

But the very first thing we are told about her is that she was barren, the ultimate indignity for ancient women. Next we learn that with Abraham she left Ur, a city of an advanced civilization, and perhaps a twenty-room house, to dwell all the rest of her days in a tent.

She was so beautiful that husband Abraham at least twice feared for his life because of her charms. She was generous, although hasty, in giving to Abraham her maid Hagar as a concubine so that there would be a descendant. (Then that feisty

86

lady blamed poor Abraham because of Hagar's insurgent attitude; triangles never work!)

But *God* blessed her and made a covenant with her concerning her own motherhood, changing her name from Sarai, meaning "princess," to Sarah, meaning "queen or mother of princes." Even so, when the angels came for brunch and told Abraham, who was ninety-eight, and Sarah, who was eighty-nine, that they would have a son the following year, she reacted with explosive amusement: "Shall I, who have long since ceased to menstruate, have the pleasure of a child by my lord who is also too old to give me one?" (See Genesis 18:12.)

It was, of course, an outlandish prediction; earlier, when God told Abraham the same news, he fell flat on his face with laughter.

God was not offended with their hilarity, for he named the coming son Isaac, which means "laughter." Perhaps he, too, enjoyed the fun of what he was about to perform!

And he did as he promised. Not only did Sarah conceive and bear Isaac, but she was able to nurse him, probably for the customary three years.

At Isaac's weaning feast Sarah saw Ishmael, Hagar's son, ridiculing Isaac. In maternal outrage, her fiery nature asserted itself again. "That boy has got to go!" she told Abraham.

And although this was grievous to Abraham, God agreed with Sarah. God told Abraham: "In all that Sarah hath said unto thee, hearken unto her voice; for in Isaac shall thy seed be called" (Genesis 21:12).

Sarah's biography does not even end with her burial in the cave of Macpelah, which was to become ancestral, but with the tender comment that after Isaac took his bride Rebekah into his mother's tent and loved her, he "was comforted after his mother's death" (Genesis 24:67). What a woman was this, so marvelously clothed with strength and honor that her grown son, three years after her death, needed the release from grief which marriage brought!

Hundreds of years later, by the Spirit's inspiration, Peter

identified Sarah among "holy women" who had the "inward adorning and beauty of the hidden person of the heart, with the incorruptible and unfading charm of a gentle and peaceful spirit, which . . . is very precious in the sight of God" (1 Peter 3:4, Amp.).

Peter remembers that she called her husband "lord" (when she laughed about the coming child) and commends her for adapting herself to her husband as secondary and dependent to him.

Besides her outer garments of fine linen and purple, the Proverbs woman had the inward adorning of strength, honor, dignity, nobility, and respect. Moffatt translated, "Strong and secure is her position."

I believe that we are seeing a maturing process in this unfolding description of the Proverbs woman. Earlier she reinforced herself by girding her loins and strengthening her arms. Now strength and honor become such an essential part of her character that the Word says they *are* her clothing. These two words, common in our language, have astonishing biblical meanings. "Strength" means might, security, and majesty and is most commonly used in the Old Testament in reference to God. It's translated "power," for example, in "Power belongeth unto God" (Psalm 62:11).

Likewise "honor" usually describes the Almighty and is variously translated as glory, majesty, beauty, and excellency. "Honor and majesty are before him" (Psalm 96:6).

Long before the term "self-esteem" came into use, the Proverbs woman had it. In the light of her accomplishments, we could say that she deserved to.

But accomplishments alone will not produce self-esteem, else no business tycoon or learned Ph.D. or Hollywood star would ever commit suicide.

I submit that the Proverbs lady found it necessary to win through some of life's low blows in order to find that inner sanctum of strength and honor.

One dismal evening a few years ago my friend Lucille finally realized that her marriage was dead; with this revelation came a sense of total rejection. "I felt absolutely worthless," she said. "I was big, I was awkward, I was ugly. If my husband who had loved me didn't want me, certainly no one else did. I poured out this anguish to God and picked up my Bible. Sitting on the floor, aimlessly I began reading in the back a section on the history of the English Bible and came to a story so beautiful that after ten years it is still difficult for me to read it without weeping."

The story was of Caedmon, a humble Saxon cowherd, who became a lay brother in an abbey where the brothers were asked to sing vespers. He, however, always fled to the stables because he could not sing. One time he fell asleep and dreamed that One stood by him who said, "Caedmon, sing me a song."

"Lord, I cannot sing," Caedmon replied.

"Nevertheless," he said, "thou canst sing to me."

Caedmon started to sing, and so beautiful was his song that when Lady Hilda of the Abbey heard of it, she instructed the priests to tell stories to Caedmon, who sang them in the Anglo-Saxon of his day.

"I cried and cried over this simple but moving story," Lucille went on. "Caedmon, too, felt worthless. But Jesus *accepted* him, *just as he was*; moreover he turned that ugliness into something beautiful and useful. That night it was Jesus accepting me.

"That was Step One to my healing of rejection. Step Two came within the hour as I began reading Psalm 139. I lingered over the fourteenth verse, and it performed the miracle of healing in my wounded, rejected spirit with its deep inferiority complex. 'I will praise thee; for I am fearfully and wonderfully made: marvelous are thy works.'

"By this time the tears were gone and I said, 'Lord, I will *never again* disparage this being that you have created.' From that moment to this day I am to myself a worthwhile person. Before, I would run myself down constantly in my conversation with others. Whether I was hoping someone would contradict me and bolster my failing ego or whether I thought if I criticized myself first, the other person wouldn't have a chance—I don't know. But to my knowledge, never again did I degrade myself. I was something that God had made.

"A year later my divorce lawyer said to me, 'I want to warn you that you'll go through a period of feeling rejected and absolutely worthless.'

"I said, 'No, I've already been through that and the Lord has taken care of it.' He looked skeptical. But I knew!"

By the time I met Lucille a few months later, she was already clothed with strength and honor—a soft-voiced, lovely, competent woman with an engaging sense of humor.

Hannah, too, as we've noted, suffered greatly for many years. But when she and her husband brought Samuel to dedicate to the Lord, she burst into song: "In the Lord I now hold my head high" (1 Samuel 2:1, NEB).

Whatever our past sins, our present circumstances, or our future prospects, I am absolutely convinced that each of us is *always* entitled to hold her head high in the Lord.

As I have prayed over this chapter, God repeatedly has brought to my attention an obscure woman in Scripture whom I'd never before noted: Rebekah's nurse, Deborah. She is first alluded to when Rebekah's family sent her away to become Isaac's wife, with the nurse accompanying her (Genesis 24:59). She is mentioned only once more, this time by name, on the occasion of her death: "But Deborah Rebekah's nurse died, and she was buried beneath Beth-el under an oak" (Genesis 35:8).

The death of Rebekah herself is not recorded and may have occurred earlier. But Jacob and all of his household paused in Beth-el to bury this woman who took care of him and Esau. An indication of their regard is that her grave marker, the oak, was named "a place of weeping." I believe that magnificence and majesty were her clothing. We do not have to be "great" to be so clothed.

Paul cautions us against thinking more highly of ourselves than we ought to think, but that carries the built-in assumption that we have a right to think *something* of ourselves. On this side of Calvary, we may remember that Jesus died for us; consequently the worth of each of us is incalculable.

The Proverbs woman placed her husband's welfare first and thus qualified as a true daughter of Sarah. But that's not all Peter

said. We may also be Sarah's daughters if we let nothing ter-
rify us.

And the Proverbs woman wasn't even afraid of growing old!
The phrase, "and she shall rejoice in time to come," is best
translated, "she laughs at the future" (Proverbs 31:25, Berk.), or
"she has no fear of old age" (TLB).

That's easier said than done!

All of my adult life I felt slightly superior to women who
bemoaned advancing years. None of the birthdays ever
bothered me—until I approached fifty. All of a sudden, "half
century" was illuminated on my mind's marquee, and I felt over
the hill. Way over. I even dreamed one afternoon (daytime naps,
yet!) that I was twenty-eight, and woke up with a cold terror that
it wasn't so. It wasn't the age that bothered me so much, I think,
as the insidious voice of the adversary telling me I hadn't ac-
complished enough to be that old.

So I really had to seek the Lord for a more wholesome out-
look. Would you believe the daily newspaper was my first source
of help? On my birthday (God knew the date), "Today's Prayer,"
which I rarely read, said: "Dear Lord, birthdays are one of your
beautiful gifts to us. Let us thank you for the opportunity of
turning one year older, growing in wisdom, strength, and gentleness."

And Lucille helped. She told me that the Lord had recently
said to her: "Sixty is a *wonderful* age." And since then she could
hardly wait to get there to see what good things God has in store.

I reasoned that if sixty is wonderful, fifty can't be too bad.

Recently I was comforted when I read Evelyn Christenson's
statement in her book, *Lord Change Me*, that it took a lot of
courage for her to turn fifty!

Besides the matter of age, perhaps there is an economic aspect to be utilized in laughing at tomorrow. Jesus said we were
not to be anxious concerning our food or clothing because our
heavenly Father will likewise provide for us.

I begin to comprehend the beauty of his promise as I watch
some of our friends respond to their Lord's calling to "live by
faith." I've observed, too, that it's easier to read about it in books

after it's all been provided than it is to experience along the way; for the piles of bills sometimes *appear* taller than the Lord's promises, and due dates have a red-inked urgency.

But the Lord does keep his Word, and what he commands he enables. Recently I witnessed part of an exciting chain of events in the lives of our friends on the faith route.

Priscilla, in Minneapolis, came up to a hundred dollar car insurance renewal, which she did not have, at the same time the Lord was directing her to fly halfway across the continent to visit Oregon friends and then us. At the last possible moment, after her human efforts had failed to raise the amount, a phone call came.

A few days before, a young friend with three small children received the shattering news that her husband wished to leave them. She cried out to Jesus, "Lord, if anybody in the whole world cares about me, please let me know."

The following day her parents, who lived several hours away, drove unexpectedly to her home, bringing her an early birthday gift—a check for $1,000, although they are not wealthy people. They had not known of their daughter's predicament or prayer. Thanking them, the young woman said, "One-tenth of this is the Lord's, so I'll send it to Priscilla." Then she phoned.

This helped clear the way for Priscilla's Oregon visit, at which she learned that her hostess had recently prayed, "God, you sent messengers to people in Bible times; can you please send someone to me?"

Here in Arizona with us, Priscilla felt strongly that on a particular day we should visit Olga and Don although she had never met them—and we both had such uncomfortable colds that we ached in every sinus.

Olga and Don, too, live by faith (Don recently left Fairbanks just four years short of retirement to supervise a new Christian day school in Arizona). I put together a bag of groceries and Priscilla took the last ten dollars of her bank account, along with a box of almond bark which she hadn't yet given away. It wasn't too surprising to learn that our friends greatly needed the special encouragement the Lord had prepared Priscilla to give.

Nor was I surprised to learn that every item I bagged was much needed in Olga's nearly bare cupboard. It did bless us all when Priscilla gave Don the ten dollars and learned their gas gauge read empty, so they couldn't have made it to school the next day without it.

But what really took our breath away was Olga's reaction when she opened the box of almond bark and got all teary with joy. Back in Alaska, their very special family treat had been occasionally to order almond bark from a candy store in Anchorage! Now the Lord had given them some again.

I love serving a God who supplies all our needs, plus bonuses. With him as my Quartermaster, I believe I, too, can learn to laugh at the future.

Because these two words, strength and honor, are so frequently used to describe the Almighty, I believe we can take special delight in considering them our clothing. But they must come from God's wardrobe. Trying to select our own garments will only put us on a "Worst Dressed List," for our own righteousness is as filthy rags—and even the best anti-perspirant can't take care of that.

But the Lord's styles are impressive: "Therefore, as God's chosen, set apart and enjoying His love, clothe yourselves with tenderness of heart, kindliness, humility, gentleness, patient endurance. . . . But crown it all with love" (Colossians 3:12, 14, Berk.).

When I put on these garments of grace, along with strength and honor, I know they will be a perfect fit because Jesus has tailored them just for me.

SIXTEEN
Her Wise Tongue Is Kind

*She openeth her mouth with wisdom; and in her
tongue is the law of kindness.* Proverbs 31:26

At last the Proverbs woman has earned the right to say something!

We have learned a great deal about her actions, her attitudes, and her mental processes. Now we find that she is wisely articulate.

Being wise is more than knowing facts; it consists in knowing how they should be arranged to do the most good. The account of Joseph's interpretation of Pharaoh's dreams is an example. The facts, as God revealed them to Joseph, were that a seven-year famine was coming. Wisdom was displayed when Joseph advised Pharaoh how to prepare for it.

But wisdom is not only knowing what to do but also understanding what not to do—and when. When Ruth asked permission of Naomi to earn their living by gleaning in the fields, Naomi answered, "Go, my daughter." But after Ruth returned from her midnight visit to Boaz at the threshing floor, Naomi said to Ruth, "Sit still, my daughter . . . for the man will not be in rest, until he have finished the thing this day" (Ruth 3:18).

Several Bible women were called wise. One whose story appears in 2 Samuel 20:16–22 has always intrigued me. Sheba was a disagreeable fellow who tried to usurp David's kingship. When David heard of it, he sent Joab, his commander, and an army after Sheba, who took refuge in the city of Abel.

Consequently Joab started to besiege the city, forgetting or ignoring the fact that the law required an army to first offer a city terms of peace (Deuteronomy 20:10).

But a wise woman of the city called out to demand an interview with Joab.

"Are you Joab?" she called.

"I am," he answered.

"Hear my words," she ordered.

Joab replied, "I am listening."

First she had to get his attention!

Then the woman gave Joab a thumbnail history of her city, which was so renowned for its wisdom that arbitrators were frequently chosen from among its citizenry. "Why," she pressed her point, "do you want to destroy us who are part of the Lord's inheritance?"

Brave Joab backed down. "Never would I want to destroy!" (He forgot that on his way to Abel he had just plunged a dagger through Amasa.) "But we must have Sheba who has threatened King David." (If he'd only said so in the first place, he might have saved his army the labor of building siege mounds and battering rams—plus a good deal of the taxpayers' money.)

"You shall have Sheba's head thrown to you over the wall," this wise woman promised. (She knew that would be positive identification.)

And she was able to deliver on that promise, for she "went unto all the people in her wisdom," overcoming their natural sympathy for a fugitive refugee. And they did toss Sheba's head down to Joab.

It seems such a simple thing as we read it—to eliminate one offender instead of razing an entire city—that we wonder why it took a wise woman to think of it. And yet I wonder how often we suffer needlessly because we are not wise enough to discern a basic problem and deal with it instead of tearing up a whole household or community. (And there are, of course, several ways of dealing with problems besides beheading!)

When I was in the eighth grade, I announced that I was not going to high school or college because I was sick of school. I knew how much my parents valued education, and I suspect that I wasn't very sincere in my protests, but was simply being perverse. This went on for some time, while my parents patiently explained and extolled the advantages of further training. Then one day I came home from school to find Aunt Lila visiting; she and Mother were calmly discussing all the housework I would be able to help with the following year when I was not in school. I disliked housework, of course, even more than I thought I hated school, which I'm sure they knew.

They opened their mouths with wisdom—and I never said another word about discontinuing my education!

Wise words can be life changing. When Belshazzar desecrated the temple vessels with a drunken banquet, and the fingers of a man's hand wrote strange words on the wall, he turned white with alarm.

But the wise queen mother, a senior citizen with a good memory, told the king and his cabinet about Daniel, in whom dwelt the Spirit of God and of wisdom, so they called him in to interpret the writing.

But wisdom is not possessed only by those with gray hair. A young girl, servant in the household of Naaman the Syrian, passed the word that a man in Israel could heal him of leprosy. It was a simple, forthright statement. But the results altered Naaman's life!

"The tongue of the wise brings healing" and "A word spoken at the right moment, how good it is!" (Proverbs 12:18; 15:23, Amp.).

The beautiful part about wisdom is that it's not limited by I.Q. There is a natural wisdom which some folks seem to have more of than others—it used to be called "horse sense." (Somebody then called it stable thinking.) But there is also God's kind of wisdom. Even as a young captive, Daniel and his three companions were noted for "knowledge and skill in all learning and wisdom" (Daniel 1:17), but when an additional supply was needed, God sent it Special Delivery.

Years later, after Daniel petitioned God for his nation, Gabriel appeared with the present: "Daniel, this time I have come to give you insight and understanding."

Our ladies' Bible study was examining the story of the impoverished widow whose two sons were about to be impounded by her creditors and whose jar miraculously filled with enough oil to pay all her bills. In my preparation I was sure I had extracted every significance from Elisha's orders for her to do such a stupid thing as borrow a lot of jars from neighbors who undoubtedly knew she had nothing to put in them.

Then Judie quietly pointed out, "She was actually being told to increase her indebtedness." It was a beautiful and thought-provoking insight.

Later Judie told me that as a small girl she often felt dumb (I'd never have guessed!) and so she had made it a lifelong prayer, "Lord, give me wisdom."

He is granting her request.

James wrote that God wants to give us wisdom without scolding us for needing to ask. Having invited us to help ourselves, the Holy Spirit then describes its ingredients: "But the wisdom that comes from heaven is first of all pure and full of quiet gentleness. Then it is peace-loving and courteous. It allows discussion and is willing to yield to others; it is full of mercy and good deeds. It is wholehearted and straightforward and sincere" (James 3:17, TLB).

The Proverbs woman had that heavenly wisdom, for "the law of kindness" was "in her tongue."

As a young person, I really wanted to be clever, a desire which I'm now certain often made me obnoxious. I wanted to obey the Lord and to be good because I knew it was smart to be good— but I surely wished to do so with distinction.

Somewhere along the way my indwelling Guest has changed that goal, and I find that now I desire, more than any other quality of which I'm aware, to be kind. Occasionally some of the harsh words I have spoken in disciplining my children (the firm ones don't bother, just the unkind ones) or in relating to my husband sting across my memory and cause me such regret that

I must quickly commit them to Jesus, the Reconciler. Sometimes yet in haste or irritation I speak unkindness to members of my family so that I need to say, "I'm sorry." (They are so generous in forgiving me.) But I *aim* toward kindness.

Often I'm impressed by the lovely change in Martha of Bethany. Looking in on one of Christ's early visits to her home, we see her all sweaty and flustered because sister Mary was listening to Jesus instead of helping her with the work. And Martha's complaint was, by implication, as unkind to the Master as it was to Mary. But when Jesus with great gentleness said, "Martha, Martha," which really meant "Martha, my dear," and then explained that Mary had chosen more wisely, Martha learned something.

So the next time Jesus came, following the death of their brother Lazarus, Martha got to Jesus first! But after she heard him say, "*I* am the resurrection, and the life" (John 11:25), she went to Mary and whispered, "Jesus is asking for you, too." Now we didn't *hear* Jesus make that request, but I like Martha's lovely kindness in making certain that she shared him with her sister.

Recently some of my friends attended a fun and fellowship retreat. For that specific occasion, the leaders made a decree: "No negative humor allowed." That started me thinking about what a pernicious habit adult cut-downs, even in fun, can be. My psychiatrist husband told me that teasing can often be a veiled expression of disapproval or hostility.

I used to be an expert at the "grand slam." It started when I was a girl, and I used to enjoy the returns, too. I still remember how funny I thought it was when my rural schoolmate Howard replied to one of my arrows with, "You're so homely you have to sneak up on the water pail to get a drink!" (My kids tell me the modern version is, "You're so ugly your mother had to stand across the room and feed you with a slingshot!")

But as an adult I've decided there must be a better way to be funny, and these days I'm trying to learn build-ups rather than put-downs. I've remembered something my mother learned from a family with whom she lived as she worked her way through high school. "Never," instructed Mrs. Roadman, "let a stranger say nicer things about your family than you do."

The family's kindness involved more than words, Mother recalls. The father, who later became Dr. Roadman, president of Sioux City's Morningside College, was then a Methodist pastor in an Iowa town. One Sunday evening, as a special loving surprise, their little daughter got up early and pressed her daddy's trousers. But since it was her first attempt, she pressed them the wrong way, with the creases on the sides. Rather than hurt his little girl, Pastor Roadman wore them as they were up to his pulpit that day.

In consequence, although I grew up in a cowboy culture (where if someone really liked another, he made a game of insulting him), I also grew up with parents who were quick to praise for good things we did. (Behavior modification experts have recently discovered the value of positive reinforcers!)

Not everyone was so blessed. I have a friend, the blue-ribbon variety in every way, whose parents presumably felt they would be pandering to the sin of pride if ever they expressed approbation. The only way she knew she pleased her parents was if they *didn't* criticize. She remembers playing a part in a school play which caused many friends, neighbors, and teachers to exclaim over her performance; but though she yearned for some word from her parents, they made no comment.

Then as a young adult, away working, she sacrificed a vacation while her mother was ill to give their farm home its annual spring cleaning—the stem-to-stern kind in which walls are scrubbed, rugs cleaned, and everything laundered except the pigs. When her mother came home from the hospital, my friend proudly took her on tour of the gleaming house. The mother made only one statement: "You got the transom curtain on upside down."

Sharing that heartache years later, my friend wept at the remembrance. Happily, she herself has learned better. It was her much-needed word of praise to me many years ago which initiated our valued friendship.

I was surprised to discover that for the Proverbs woman the "law of kindness" was not just a figure of speech but was exactly that—a law. The same word describes the Torah and the Pentateuch and means "statute." Perhaps it can be called the eleventh commandment, and the only one which survives as such in the New Testament, where Jesus said the whole law could be summed up in loving.

Being kind is not an elective; it's a requirement.

Kindness is not, of course, necessarily always pleasant. It's more than helping sweet old ladies across the street or cuddling freshly talcumed, cooing babies—or even saying nice things to people. The Word tells us that "Punishment that hurts chases evil from the heart" (Proverbs 20:30, TLB), and as "an ornament of fine gold is a wise reprover to an ear that listens and obeys" (Proverbs 25:12, Amp.).

My dearest friends have needed to reprove me, sometimes firmly; but because I knew they loved me and were obeying our Lord, I have been able to accept their correction as the kindness it really was. Similarly, on a few occasions I have felt it necessary to admonish.

And frequently—as often as seventy times seven—kindness may involve the hardest thing of all: forgiveness.

A year ago my youngest sister, a bright, active businesswoman in her thirties, was deliberately shot with a .357 magnum by her teenage stepdaughter. As Loisanne lay alone in her blood across the doorstep of her beautiful suburban home with her lower body paralyzed and one arm shattered at the elbow, she noticed how blue and beautiful the sky was. She thought that if she died, she would not be able to tell her family how much she really loved them (we've all been doing more of that since then), and she was concerned that she be found and removed before her sons returned to see her in that condition.

After nearly an hour, her assailant returned, Loisanne assumed to finish killing her. But my sister spoke to her kindly, begging her to phone for help, and then she said: "I don't hate you; I forgive you."

With those words, I believe, Loisanne set in motion the divine forces which not only kept her miraculously alive but which continue to work for her good. Today she is a paraplegic, confined to a wheelchair. She's had numerous operations, but still carries the slug in her spine. Constant pain and inconvenience are such a part of her life, that her initial forgiving spirit is often sorely tried—as it is for all who love her. But I am convinced that her forgiveness will endure, for the benefit of all involved.

Jesus not only *gives* us wisdom, the Bible says, but he *is* our wisdom (1 Corinthians 1:30).

Likewise God, who *is* love, expressed that love in the kindness of Jesus: "But when the time came for the kindness and love of God our Savior to appear, then he saved us . . . by washing away our sins and giving us the new joy of the indwelling Holy Spirit whom he poured out upon us with wonderful fullness . . . all because of his great kindness" (Titus 3:4–7, TLB).

How do we acquire wisdom or kindness or any of the other Christlike virtues we greatly desire?

Sometimes as we earnestly ask in faith, our Father gives us a special, immediate, divine dispensation. Recently I was wronged by someone I trusted and cared for; moreover that wrong involved leading a young person into error. As Pastor Dave and I visited and prayed one afternoon, I realized with horror that unforgiveness and hatred were trying to take root in my heart. With Dave as witness, I quickly said to God, "Help!"

A couple of days later my "enemy's" name came unexpectedly to my attention; suddenly I was filled with love and a desire to pray for her, which continue to this moment.

But there are still other negative qualities I struggle over, and positive traits I would like which are not yet present in my life.

In 1852 Nathaniel Hawthorne published "The Great Stone Face," a story which tells of a rock formation resembling the features of a man's face. As a young boy, Ernest heard from his mother a legend that one day someone native to the area would return to bestow noble and inspiring deeds on the people of his home community. He would be known by the resemblance of his visage to that face on the mountain. In the evenings, as Ernest gazed at the configuration, he hoped in the prophecy and felt a kinship to the likeness he saw.

Over the years a millionnaire, a general, and a politician came back home; each in turn was acclaimed as the expected hero. But neither their lives nor their faces resembled the Great Stone Face; and as Ernest turned away in disappointment, he would look again at the original and it would encourage him to keep on believing.

Meanwhile his own modest but careful living brought him to the position of preacher to his own people, who gradually came to look to him for advice and wisdom.

One evening a visiting poet accompanied Ernest as he stood outdoors to speak to a gathering of his friends and neighbors. Hawthorne wrote: "His words had power, because they accorded with his thoughts; and his thoughts had reality and depth, because they harmonized with the life which he had always lived". . . . The poet, as he listened, felt that the being and character of Ernest were a nobler strain of poetry than he had ever written. . . . At a distance, but distinctly to be seen, high up in the golden light of the setting sun, appeared the Great Stone Face, with hoary mists around it, like the white hairs around the brow of Ernest. . . .

"At that moment, in sympathy with a thought which he was about to utter, the face of Ernest assumed a grandeur of expression, so imbued with benevolence, that the poet, by an irresistible impulse, threw his arms aloft, and shouted,

"'Behold! Behold! Ernest is himself the likeness of the Great Stone Face!'"

For me this story graphically illustrates what is probably my favorite verse: "But we all, with open face beholding as in a glass the glory of the Lord, are changed into the same image from glory to glory, even as by the Spirit of the Lord" (2 Corinthians 3:18).

If I will do the beholding—of the glory of Jesus—his Spirit will do the changing. And increasingly I will become like him.

Hallelujah, again and again.

SEVENTEEN
She Is Not Idle

She looketh well to the ways of her household,
and eateth not the bread of idleness.
Proverbs 31:27

Our heroine has done so much good for her husband that he sits in the gates. She has prospered with a field, a vineyard, and a fabric and girdle business; furthermore she can afford to wear fine linen and purple.

To her household she has given meat (early!), an example of fearlessness, and warm clothing. By this time one would imagine her nearly ready for retirement or at least delegating most of her duties to the maids.

Not so. "She watches carefully all that goes on throughout her household, and is never lazy" (Proverbs 31:27, TLB). She continues to be diligent, as obviously she has always been. I suspect that a woman of her consequence had a large and diverse household, besides the children which are later mentioned and the maids we already know about. With a husband in politics, she may have done lots of hostessing; and she likely had business obligations of her own.

We know how complex the typical modern housewife's schedule can be also. I vividly recall the afternoon I had to pick up my three children from two schools and then drive them to three swimming lessons, two birthday parties, and a church activity—with a leaking radiator hose which kept stalling the car.

Yesterday at a luncheon a friend told me about one of her acquaintances who, on blanks where she is to state her occupation, writes, "Director of Household Management, Finance, and Transportation." Thousands of us concur. And a single woman in an efficiency apartment may be just as thoroughly involved in her business household or her spiritual family.

Nevertheless, the Proverbs woman was not Mrs. Nosy. (The New Testament has some uncomplimentary things to say about busybodies, as in 1 Peter 4:15, where they are ranked with murderers and thieves.) The term, "looketh well," means, rather, to observe, peer into the distance, and keep the watch.

And the noun, "ways," refers to a procession or going, not to manners or actions. We have a picture then, not of an interfering fussbudget who constantly gets hung up on minor details, but of an organizer who observes trends. She understands the directions in which members of her household are going. She is aware of their intentions and desires even if they occasionally track mud into the house, leave their books at school, type a sloppy letter or forget to put an announcement in the church bulletin.

Sometimes this will make her a watchdog. She will "feel" that things are not right with a child, an employee, an associate, or another believer. When one of my daughters was a second grader, she invited a new classmate home to play one afternoon. The playmate struck me at once as being somewhat precocious, and after a few minutes I felt I needed to go into the room where they were playing dolls, for they had closed the door against a possible brotherly invasion. I found that they had just undressed themselves. I quickly corrected the situation and saved the discussion for later with my own child; but I learned something: children's closed doors, especially when others are present, need to be opened from time to time.

Not long ago I also "felt" that a beautiful young friend, recently divorced, needed attention; a long-distance call confirmed this fact—and refreshed us both in the love of our Lord.

The Philippian church may have been Paul's favorite; he used more terms of endearment toward them and applied less correction than to any of the others he wrote to. But even there, problems existed; for he needed to "beseech" two competent and energetic women, Euodias and Syntyche, to stop quarreling. He didn't phrase it as such; tactfully he urged them to "be of the same mind in the Lord" (Philippians 4:2). (We *can* be agreed in Jesus, even if we don't see eye to eye about how to fold the napkins for the church supper.)

Further, Paul "entreated" another of the believers to help these women; he asked him to assume the role of restorer. He did this because all of these people, including the warring women, were dearly beloved and longed for, his joy and his crown (Philippians 4:1).

Our own "smarts" are often not sufficient to keep us ahead, or even abreast, of the way things are going with our households. Returning from a foster parents' conference, my friend Julie commented: "I'm not comfortable with the idea that we always have to out-psych kids. It seems to me that we have to live normally and trust the Lord to direct us a whole lot."

One of my favorite people has shared with me how that happened for her. As a young pastor's wife, she was part-time church secretary, leaving her three children home a few hours a week with an older church lady who was experienced and loving. But one day when my friend came home, her sitter was troubled. "I really hate to mention it," the lady said, "but when I came yesterday, I had a ten-dollar bill in my purse. When I got home, it was gone. Your boy was the only one here, and I'm sure he must have taken it."

That evening during dishes my friend talked to her eight-year-old. "Did you take money from our friend's purse?"

The little boy turned his large, innocent brown eyes directly onto his mother's and solemnly assured her: "Oh no, Mommie. I wouldn't do a thing like that. I know it's wrong to steal, and I love our sitter."

"He was so convincing," my friend told me, "that I *fully* believed him and decided there must be another explanation for the missing money. Then all of a sudden, I began to sob aloud.

Great big tears ran down my face and into the dishwater. I was completely astonished at myself, but I couldn't stop.

"My son stared at me for a moment and then he ran to me, confessing, 'I did take the money, Mommie, and I'm so sorry. I'll never do it again!'

"I knew at once that it was the Holy Spirit weeping through me. Our boy was just beginning to rebel and do serious mischief. It was crucial for him to know that God could expose sin; more important, because he loved me, those tears so touched his heart that he could truly repent. And from that moment on, I was assured that the Holy Spirit would help me with him."

Today that young man, nearly through college, has won many kinds of honors, has demonstrated unusual anointing as a soul-winner, and has a mature understanding of what it means to be God's servant.

Perhaps looking well to our household's ways will mean that we can do nothing more than pray. But that could be everything! Is it possible that if there had been time for a fellowship to become established, someone could have prayed for Sapphira and she and her husband would not have dropped dead with lies on their lips?

Several years ago I needed to intercede for a beloved friend in a time of deep trial and spiritual slippage. Very recently she shared with me: "Once during that period in my life I *felt* an angel. I did not see him, though I looked; but as I turned quickly, I bumped him with my elbow. There was nobody anywhere near me at the time, and I knew the angel was there to protect me."

With tears, she added, "Perhaps if we were more fully *aware* of how God sends his angels as ministering spirits, we could pray for our friends more effectively." (See Hebrews 1:14.)

Hearing this, I was reverently reminded that in my striving to be the kind of woman God wants, I am not alone. All of heaven's hosts are arrayed at his command and available according to my needs—and the needs of those I pray for.

Careful observation of the ways of those we're concerned with will most certainly reveal that each is unique. The only mold that

God ever made was the one that will conform us to the image of his son—and that one is different for each person.

Sometimes I've been a slow learner on that score. Our eldest was never a "food fussy." Our son's first rational speech every morning has always been, "What's for breakfast?" But then came Nora, and after she passed babyhood, she simply wasn't hungry when she first woke up.

Everyone needs a good breakfast, right? So I pushed and coaxed and nagged. Once we were traveling and there wasn't time for her to get hungry before our restaurant breakfast stop. So Nora and I had a terrible time over her toast and eggs. At that point my wise husband intervened, assuring me that she would very likely not perish of malnutrition in the next few hours if all she had was orange juice. What a relief! For all of us.

My father grew up in an atmosphere, which he absorbed, of extreme profanity. When he and Mother knelt in their farm kitchen to accept the Lord, one of the sins my father most sorrowfully repented of was that he had spent so many years cursing the name of his now-beloved Lord. He prayed that he might never do so again—and despite the habits of years and the obstreperous behavior of his cows, no oath ever again escaped his lips.

But I have a friend who also loves her Savior with a depth and a spontaneity which continually refreshes. As a new Christian, she stubbed her foot so painfully that she let loose a string of epithets—and then was nearly crushed by grief over her lapse. The Lord forgave her, of course, and will one day deliver her, if he hasn't already.

As I observe carefully the ways of my household, I need to remind myself constantly that I am not to exert pressures solely according to my personal preferences but I am to promote *God's* best manner of going for each person.

Such observation does not always reveal negatives; sometimes commendation is in order. God gave Paul a most exquisite gift for spotting good qualities. In many ways the Corinthians were rather a sorry lot; they had problems with quarreling and incest and stealing and getting drunk at communion, besides not using spiritual gifts in an orderly manner. But Paul opens his first letter to them by being thankful that Jesus had given them God's grace, that they were enriched in everything, and that they excelled in the gifts the Holy Spirit had bestowed on them.

The Colossians, who were in danger of falling prey to the teachings of the sophists, were the mind expanders of that day. Even though they did not properly regard the person and power of Jesus Christ, Paul expressed gratitude for their faith in Jesus, their love for one another, and their hope of heaven.

Paul thanked Philemon, a slave owner, for his love toward *all* saints!

When King Josiah of Judah was twenty-six, the book of God's Law, long unread and disregarded, was discovered. As the king read it, he was aghast. He said to his cabinet members, "Go, ask the Lord for me, for the people and all Judah in regard to what this book that was found says. The Lord's anger blazing against us is so great because our fathers refused to listen to what this book says and to do all that is written about us" (2 Kings 22:13, Beck).

To Huldah the prophetess was revealed God's understanding of the ways of the household of Judah, and she told Josiah's messengers that punishment would come upon the people who had willfully disobeyed. But she sent word to King Josiah that because his heart was open, tender, and humble toward the Lord, his own lifetime would be peaceful. God looked past his actions to the direction of his heart and spoke good to him.

We, too, may be either instruments of correction or comfort to our households.

One of the things I like best about the character of the Proverbs woman is that she is basically positive. Only four "nots" are listed. She does her husband "not evil." Her candle goes "not out." She is "not afraid." Fourth and last, she does "not eat the bread of idleness." Even these "nots" are but negative expressions of positive qualities.

Biblical numerology is one interesting way to examine the Scriptures. Four is considered the number representing earth.

On the fourth day creation of material matter was completed; the earth has four seasons, four directions. The four gospels describe Christ's earthly life. These four negatives describing the Proverbs woman, as well as the fact that the word "household" occurs four times, tell me that she is meant as a helpful example to all of us earthly females. She is not merely a hopelessly perfect ideal to whom we might as well wave goodbye.

Certainly there are dangers in idleness. The *Amplified Bible* reads, "and the bread of idleness [gossip, discontent and self-pity] she will not eat." I don't know whether Miriam grew idle or not, but an incident in her life conveys a strong warning. Both she and Aaron jealously attacked Moses because of his Egyptian wife; they implied that they should have greater status because their gifts were as great as those of Moses.

But the Eternal was listening. Quickly he summoned the three siblings to the tent of meeting where he appeared in a pillar of cloud. He reaffirmed the greatness of Moses and sternly rebuked Aaron and Miriam. When he departed, Miriam was a leper. I'm not sure why only Miriam was stricken, when both she and Aaron were guilty, unless it was that she was going to need Aaron as her intercessor. But I do understand how God feels about vicious gossip, especially that leveled against his chosen leaders.

The opposite of idleness is diligence, and the Bible has a great deal to say about that. Early on, the nation of Israel was instructed: "And you must think constantly about these commandments I am giving you today. You nust teach them to your children and talk about them when you are at home or out for a walk; at bedtime and the first thing in the morning. Tie them on your finger, wear them on your forehead, and write them on the doorposts of your house!" (Deuteronomy 6:6–9, TLB).

Jesus was thorough. After he had healed the man born blind who was then cast out of the synagogue for refusing to label his Healer a sinner, the Lord looked him up. Gently and clearly he told the forsaken man that he was the Christ—a privileged occasion of acknowledgment—and the man worshiped him.

Onesiphorus was diligent enough to search for Paul in Rome until he found him, so that he might minister to Paul in prison (2 Timothy 1:16, 17).

(In the days when I had lots of ironing, I used to take comfort in knowing that Paul, too, needed to "press toward the mark"!)

But diligence doesn't mean that we have to do everything ourselves. Jesus told his disciples that when they saw the fields ready to be harvested, they were to pray for laborers—they weren't to start wielding their own scythes twenty-four hours a day. While we are not to eat the bread of idleness, neither are we to be frenetic peripatetics.

The apostles learned this quickly. Acts 5:42 tells us that daily in the Temple and in houses they ceased not to teach and preach Jesus Christ. But in the next chapter we read that they found it necessary to appoint men full of the Holy Ghost and wisdom to take care of church welfare so they could continue to give themselves to prayer and preaching.

Diligence gets results. Our eldest had a particularly difficult time with basic arithmetic. She learned to add on her fingers, but by the time she got to multiplication and division, there weren't enough fingers to do the job. Memorizing the combinations was the only solution, but it proved exceedingly difficult for her.

It took most of a summer at her grandparents' home several states away, and my mother, a retired teacher with special skills in elementary mathematics, faced a major challenge. But she persevered. She made up games and wore out flash cards, and they had combinations for breakfast, lunch, and dinner, and much of the time in between. Our daughter persevered, for she has that quality—and she loved her grandmother. Finally they conquered. And our girl made A's and B's in math from then through high school.

The Lord has some arithmetic for us to master, also. It's an exercise in addition, and he tells us that we will need diligence to work the problem. It's listed in 2 Peter 1:5–8 and reads: Faith plus virtue plus knowledge plus temperance plus patience plus godliness plus brotherly kindness plus love. The correct answer

will keep us from being either idle or unfruitful. So if we exercise diligence, we will become diligent and productive persons.
And I need that.

EIGHTEEN
Call Her Blessed

Her children arise up, and call her blessed.
Proverbs 31:28

To my knowledge, Minnie Johnson was never written up in a newspaper or magazine. I did not meet her until the last three years of her earthly life. She was an excellent seamstress, cook, and housekeeper; but so are thousands of other women in Minnesota and elsewhere.

But during my acquaintance with her I came to understand that my life was touching one of God's special saints; for she had a quiet spirit that made her truly beautiful. She was not at all self-assertive, but occasionally during Sunday evening hymn request time she would ask for "I Have a Friend Who Loveth Me." Once, seated ahead of her, I could hear her elderly but still sweet soprano on the chorus: "O, hallelujah, He's my Friend! He guides me to the journey's end. He walks beside me all the way, and will bestow a crown someday."[1] I was deeply moved.

Needing a special kind of green button, I stopped by her home one afternoon. As I supposed, her ample box contained what I needed. More, she and her husband Alfred gave me delicious Swedish pastry and coffee and their unfailingly gracious hospitality. Even that day, after the first of several strokes which eventually took her Home, Minnie had a quiet comment

[1] Taken from "I Have a Friend Who Loveth Me," *The Covenant Hymnal*, No. 416. Used by permission.

of gratitude about the abundant blessings from their Lord. I knew that her life had not always been smooth—she had lost an infant child, and their farm home during the Depression; and the sheer workload of raising eight children to maturity had been heavy.

During Minnie's last hospitalization, after speech was gone and she was often extremely uncomfortable, she seemed one day to wish to communicate. A granddaughter handed her a pad and pencil, and she laboriously scrawled her final message: "God is so good."

Although earlier three of her children had been overseas and one had to fly back to his mission station in Japan on the following day, God arranged for all eight children to be present for her final celebration. They were a distinguished group—a principal, businessmen, a homemaker, a minister, and three missionaries. As they gathered with their families at the funeral home, the day before the service, they began spontaneously to sing "How Great Thou Art" and then "I Will Praise Him." Awestruck, one of the funeral directors exclaimed, "No choir on earth could sound better than that family!" He urged his partner to listen to them again that evening when they praised the Lord with music: "Let us magnify the Lord and lift up holy hands and worship him."

Daughter Priscilla told me, "To worship with my family on that occasion was one of the most fantastic experiences of my life. Not one of us had one negative thing to say about my mother. And we did not grieve, for we knew she was released from suffering and rejoicing with Jesus."

I don't think, however, that we have to wait until we die for our children to call us blessed. (Minnie's sons and daughters for many years had been lovingly attentive.) There is no indication that the Proverbs woman's children, on this first Mother's Day, were delivering a funeral eulogy.

One of my treasured memories is of the time we gave three-year-old Nora her first pair of knee socks ten years ago. She was so thrilled that all day long she kept stopping to admire their bright colors and fine, new feel. Late in the day she came into the kitchen and said, "Mommy, why don't you get *you* some knee socks?"

The day was hot and I was busy with supper and feeling every one of my forty years, so I carelessly answered, "Oh, Honey, I'm too old for knee socks."

I was totally unprepared for her reaction. Nora's blue eyes flashed vehemently as she reproved me: "Mommy, you're not old! You're new!"

Parenting is more work, and causes more suffering than any other occupation I know. And it has the greatest rewards. A loving Father puts a few of these gems in the mouths of our children as we go along, probably because he so much longs for *us* to praise *him*; and the prospect of our children's eventual "arising up" to call us blessed is indeed a lovely one.

The Proverbs woman's child-raising kit must have included more than a sense of responsibility and a dutiful supplying of proper diet and clothing. There is a suggestion of sensitivity to social graces in their "arising up," which tells me that their mother was warm, tender, and caring. Otherwise they might merely have sent a servant with a greeting scroll and another cushion or candle.

I've always loved my kids, but recently the Lord has added something which I should probably have asked him for years ago. I don't know exactly what to call it, but one of its components is an appreciation for each one, blemishes and all. A second ingredient is the ability to *enjoy* them. And I'm trying to spend at least as many words (preferably more) in love and appreciation as in correction. When we had some genuinely serious concerns with one, as I sought the Lord in prayer, he gave me only one direction: "Love that one." Since the child was being pretty difficult, loving wasn't the easiest course of action. And it did require action, for a guilty conscience made the person withdrawn and sometimes sullen. Now, however, we're seeing better communication and behavior, and more smiles.

A few years ago during another crisis, I realized that we weren't having enough fun at home. With my friends I laughed and joked, but when I was home with the children I was too often grimly involved with making good people out of them. As we sought to correct that, suppertime went much better with laughter.

Since "blessed" can be translated "happy," I believe the Proverbs woman kept a vial of laughter in her bag, too. "A merry heart doeth good like a medicine" (Proverbs 17:22), and besides being a lot easier to take, it's much cheaper!

But the word from which "blessed" derives can also be translated "straight" or "level." That suggests more than light-heartedly tripping through the tulips. Blessedness is based on integrity, in being "on the level," and every carpenter knows how important that is. Her children respected her.

She was honest with them.

She acknowledged their basic privacy.

She did not dominate their lives in every detail.

She tried to be as polite to them as she was to company.

The respect that Jesus accorded the disciples, who were his children, is our example.

Nor does one have to marry and have children to be called blessed. There will be single women in heaven with so many spiritual children that they'll have to stand in line to express their acclaim. I knew several such women in my college days: Dr. Rice, a gentle genius who helped me through my zoology labs even though I was never really sure I saw anything through the microscope other than my own eyelashes; Miss Dooley who taught me Shakespeare and Milton and much more that is not in textbooks; Miss Washburn who honed my freshman compositions; Miss Allison who lived in our dorm. Once when we salted her room with numerous alarm clocks set to ring every hour throughout the night, she arranged them all in a museum-like display, neatly labeled as though from far-off places. Through it all, she was gracious and amused.

Dr. Culver taught me world history and manners in high school and then, after earning her Ph.D., became my college instructor in education. A dozen years ago my husband and I spent a too-brief evening with her. Tears glistened as we parted and she said, "It's a good Way, Virginia."

Each of these women was even more concerned with my spiritual condition than with my intellectual development; anytime I went forward for prayer in our chapel services or needed counsel, any one of those godly ladies was available and helpful. As they say in Oklahoma, "I wouldn't take for their influence."

We don't know anything about the natural family of Priscilla and Aquila, but we do know they had a church in their house. And "having a church" in those dangerous times was undoubtedly more than prayer, hymns, announcements, and a sermon. Very likely it included nurture in the faith, such as they gave to Apollos, perhaps for long periods of time.

Paul himself must have needed a bit of mothering which apparently the mother of Rufus was willing to provide (Romans 16:13).

A missionary to Japan told me that their young converts are often expelled from their homes when they accept Christ; consequently church services frequently include a meal to which everyone contributes what he can. Some days they have only tea and rolls, but the fellowship, and the parenting of the missionaries, is vital.

God wants our concerns to extend beyond our immediate circles, for he says, "Sing, O childless woman! Break out into loud and joyful song. . . . Enlarge your house; build on additions; spread out your home! For you will soon be bursting at the seams!" (Isaiah 54:1–3, TLB).

There is a kind of enlargement of the heart which is not a disease!

In an exquisite little book titled *My Thoughts Toward You*,[2] the author, Priscilla Mohrenweiser, expresses the Lord's point of view: "My children give me joy when they are concerned about My family everywhere. They please Me when they are compassionate and are willing, when it lies within their power, to alleviate suffering. They please Me greatly when My concerns become their concerns, and thus they share in My sufferings. Then My heart rejoices because together we are sharing the

[2] From *My Thoughts Toward You.* Copyright © 1975 by PM Publications, Route One, St. Cloud, Minnesota 56301. Used by permission.

work of My Kingdom. Those who do this will one day be prepared to reign with Me."

The Virgin Mary said that all generations would call her
blessed because the Lord had done great things for her.

Jesus said of Mary of Bethany who poured a whole bottle of
expensive perfume over his head, "She will always be remembered for this deed" (Matthew 26:13, TLB). She had done great
things for God.

Ultimately those are the two most important reasons why our
children will be able to call us blessed.

Father, let them see what you have done for me and what I
have done for you.

NINETEEN
Her Husband Praises

. . . her husband also, and he praiseth her.
Many daughters have done virtuously, but thou
excellest them all. Proverbs 31:28b, 29

It's the second round of applause for the virtuous woman. Not to be outdone by his children, the lady's husband stays home from the gates long enough to add his voice.

He's not just an "also" or an echo, however. In this third and last mention of him he has the honor, as befits a statesman, of making the only directly quoted statement in the entire passage: "Many daughters have done nobly, but you transcend them all" (Proverbs 31:29, Berk.).

That's big talk! Did she really excel Miriam and Sarah and Hannah and Esther? Or does his declaration merely express the extravagance of love? (And after all those years!) Either way, his verbal valentine was good to hear.

There's a lovely mutuality here. Having put his trust in his wife at the beginning of their marriage, the husband now sees the returns on his investment and he gives her this tribute. The wife, having resolved to do him only good, now hears word of her success from him whose welfare has been her major objective.

But when he tells her that she has done virtuously, I don't believe he meant she had always done perfectly. Every woman has always had flub days. There must have been times for the Proverbs woman, too, when someone spilled olive oil on the

118

tapestry, the maids forgot to get enough milk, a child caught cold from not wearing his red flannels, or her warp did nothing but woof. In his summation, Mr. Proverbs kindly forgot those incidents.

My husband is a good forgetter, too. He doesn't remember the time I failed to put yeast in the pizza dough and after the first crunch he was moved to remark, "It is the feast of unleavened bread." Or one occasion I was running late, and I asked him before he went to work to please feed the baby who, with a mouthful of pablum, blew bubbles all over his freshly cleaned suit. (Although I'd remembered to bib the baby, I neglected to put a dropcloth on George.) And I hope he's lost count of the number of times I've locked myself out of our house or car.

I realize that a great many of the Lord's ladies today do not have husbands who will ever foreseeably recognize their efforts, or they have no husband at all. Thousands more have heard daily accusations, some made public in the torture of divorce. For all of those who sleep alone every night, as well as for those with loving mates who, being human, cannot possibly be all that they need, God has a message of exquisite comfort: "For thy Maker is thine husband; the Lord of hosts is his name. . . . For the Lord hath called thee as a woman forsaken and grieved in spirit, and a wife of youth, when thou wast refused, saith thy God" (Isaiah 54:5, 6).

Although this Scripture wasn't known to me then, I will never forget the time I really learned of my divine Husband's care. It was just after I'd been confronted with new teaching concerning the Holy Spirit's work, and my initial attitude of rejecting it resulted in a coolness toward the pastor and his wife and the entire congregation who believed it. One day my sister Pat phoned from Arizona that both of my parents were ill and in the hospital. Since we were then in Alaska, it would have been very difficult for me to go to them as I longed to do, and I was greatly concerned.

Joan, of the suspect congregation, happened to be visiting me when the phone call came, and she told the others in the fellowship. They first planned to have a special prayer meeting for my parents, but an ice storm made travel dangerous, so they formed a prayer chain instead. I did not know of this until my parents were out of danger and I phoned the pastor's wife to report.

When Elaine told me of their intercession, I was ashamed and I blurted, "Oh, I am not worthy."

There was a pause, and then in her soft southern accent Elaine said, "Honey, *Jesus* loves you!"

I cannot express the impact of those words, though I'd been hearing them for more than thirty years; and no moment of truth for me has ever been more important.

I have no idea why it took me so long to realize the love of Christ, because his Word is full of endearments. God has called us beautiful, darling, turtle-dove, the apple of his eye, and precious. The word "beloved" occurs repeatedly, more than thirty times in the Song of Solomon alone, with reference to the bride of the King, of which I am a part. To an entire nation God said, "You shall be called Hephzibah [My delight is in her]" (Isaiah 62:4, Amp.).

Furthermore, like the Proverbs husband and mine, the Lord is a Forgetter. He remembers my sin no more. (See Jeremiah 31:34.) When I explore the gallery of faith in Hebrews 11, I see a good deal more that God had forgotten by the time his Spirit painted those word pictures. He forgot the temper tantrum Moses indulged; he forgot that Isaac was duped when he blessed Jacob and Esau, and Samson's fatal weakness for women.

He identifies Rahab as a harlot but commends her faith. He names David without listing his sins of adultery and murder. And he even listed Jephthah, who really did a dumb thing when he offered to sacrifice the first creature that met him as he returned from battle (he should have known that his daughter was likely to run out to meet him). All of these and others, in spite of their lapses and failures, got A's on their report cards. (See Hebrews 11:39.)

Sometimes I think God deliberately and humorously recorded the foolishness of his children. The night before his probable execution, Peter was miraculously delivered from prison by an angel. Going at once to John Mark's home, where many people were praying, he knocked at the gate. But the damsel Rhoda, who answered the door, got so excited when she heard his voice that she forgot to let him in. (Typical teenager! But I love her for her exuberance—and the fact that she was at prayer meeting.)

The other Christians weren't very bright either, because instead of checking out Rhoda's report, they got into a theological argument with her—while Peter, still in mortal danger, continued knocking for admission!

I, too, have blundered badly. As a young girl during an evangelistic invitation, I went to a teenager whose parents had recently begun attending our church and begged her to go forward. Thoroughly embarrassed, she made no response. In later years I blushed with shame every time I remembered the inappropriateness of my actions. But after several years, having given her heart to the Lord and become a beautiful Christian, Lillian wrote to thank me for my concern on that occasion. How kind our Lord, and his children, are!

I know that I am to praise and bless the Lord—at all times. But I find it inexpressibly wonderful that he also praises me. He has said that he will bless the righteous (Psalm 5:12), and since Jesus Christ is made righteousness to me, I qualify for that blessing.

Again and again and again, Hallelujah.

TWENTY
She Fears the Lord

*Favour is deceitful, and beauty is vain: but a
woman that feareth the Lord, she shall be
praised.* Proverbs 31:30

When I was in the fourth grade, we moved to a farm near
Carthage, South Dakota. It was there that my parents were
exposed to the gospel and accepted Jesus Christ. I was immediately aware of the dramatic changes in their lives, so when
my daddy came into my room the following night and told me
that I, too, could be forgiven of my sins (which were many) and
know the Lord, I was ready. I experienced a comfort and a peace
I had never imagined in all my nine years. Besides the wonder of
that knowledge, I found the activity and togetherness of a
church fellowship to be very precious, filling out much of the
loneliness I had always known in our rural settings.

But the school was something else. A peeling, white-painted
box, it stood starkly on the prairie, accompanied only by two
smaller boxes labeled "Boys" and "Girls." There were no trees,
swings, or playground equipment except the gunny sacks we
brought from home to use for softball bases; not even a flagpole
with chain rattling in the wind rose from its premises. In the
beginning it had been euphemistically named Bluebell School,
District No. 36, but none of us ever saw a bluebell.

Cars were so infrequent on the narrow, black-dirt road that we
all rose to peer out the windows when we heard a vehicle of any
sort, and no teacher ever forbade our doing so.

But we were reprimanded if we spent too much time back at the water pail, which sat on a small oilcloth-covered table beside the enameled wash basin and bar of hand soap. That brand of soap, whatever it was, has not survived; but through the years I have sometimes caught a whiff of a similar fragrance. Like some elusive, olfactory "lost chord," it has a strange power to transport me back to that time and place. And I smell not only the soap but the other schoolroom odors—sweeping compound, pencil shavings, Carter's washable blue ink, and peanut butter sandwiches.

Once again I see the black coal stove glowing red as the icy winds tattooed frost pictures on our windows. As we huddled around it, sometimes wearing our coats and boots, I found it easier to concentrate on adjective clauses, Lewis and Clark, or even the hated "givens" and "to finds" of arithmetic.

Was I culturally disadvantaged? I think not. For one year a truly gifted teacher came to occupy that scarred desk on which sat the recess bell with the wobbly handle. She was slim and wore her graying dark hair in a bun, but there all stereotyping ended. An indefinable refinement distinguished Mrs. Larson from the many other excellent teachers I had known, though we learned little about her except that she had earlier taught for several years and now lived a few miles away with her farmer husband. She had never borne children; yet I was amazed that she understood us so thoroughly.

A devotee of the Palmer Method, Mrs. Larson wrote the most beautiful capital "L's" and "J's" I had ever seen. Inspired, we made circles and pushups with our straight pens and permanently ink-stained fingers to achieve the progression of certificates and pins for handwriting proficiency.

Mrs. Larson loved nature—especially birds—and was not afraid to talk about God the Creator. So our school became a member of the Audubon Club. We learned that the Arm and Hammer Baking Soda Company would send bird cards for the asking, so we besieged them with requests, penned in Palmer Method, of course, and written in proper form during our language classes. Studying for our weekly report on a specific bird, I would often gaze longingly at the pictures of the cardinal and the scarlet tanager, thinking that if I could ever see either, my life would surely be complete. Many years later we lived in Oklahoma where cardinals were numerous, and I reveled in their loveliness of plumage, song, and disposition. Then four years ago, during a Minnesota June, a small band of scarlet tanagers stopped briefly to feed on the hospital grounds where we lived. Breathlessly I finally beheld their iridescent beauty, better even than any picture I had ever seen. The Lord really does give us our hearts' desires!

Our teacher read different kinds of books aloud: of the fictional Lucinda who roller-skated down the streets of New York or of the real Admiral Byrd. These and others were somehow made real to us dwellers of the wind-baked prairies. I began to dream and aspire and to thrill to the cadence of words. Always she taught us values such as truthfulness and compassion, shaping our characters as well as our minds.

And she demanded our best, sometimes with startling methods. One morning she deliberately wrote on the board, "This book fell of the desk," and at the end of the day chastised us because nobody had called the error to her attention. Another time she brought to us a strange fruit, but would not tell us its name. Our curriculum for a good while that Monday morning consisted of researching until we could identify it as a kumquat. Then we were allowed to eat it, carefully noting its distinctive qualities.

When I received my first autograph book, I took it to her to have her write in, and she asked to keep it overnight. The next day I read in her flowing handwriting: "Dear Virginia, 'The fear of the Lord is the beginning of knowledge.' Proverbs 1:7. Your friend, Mrs. Julia Larson."

At first I was a little disappointed in her contribution because I had hoped she'd compliment me—though that was not her style. More, I was surprised that she knew a Scripture! And one that I hadn't yet discovered. In the fervor of our new evangelical beliefs, I was often quite outspoken at school, and I found that she belonged to a denomination I'd heard was both "liberal" and "formal." Somehow her reserve never invited discussion, however, so I just uneasily hoped the Lord would make an exception in her case and take her to heaven anyway. Finding out that she read the Bible was definitely a relief. And the verse itself became firmly lodged in my mind and heart.

When spring came our six east windows were festooned with Dutch children, tulips, and wooden windmills, and Mrs. Larson packed us into her Model A for a field trip to the county courthouse in De Smet, seventeen whole miles away. Loaded with bird books, notebooks, and lunch pails, we sat on the novelty of a freshly sprinkled green lawn, quietly, so that a new kind of bird might get himself recorded in our lists.

The next few days at school we perspired over a booklet recording the excursion. Howard in the eighth grade could draw best, but I was chosen to write the main report. The younger pupils colored, cut and pasted, and when it was all finished, Mrs. Larson read it to us while we glowed with the pride of achievement.

Later that day she came unexpectedly to my desk. Something special in her wise brown eyes captured and held my complete attention. "Virginia," she said in a voice vibrant but with quiet authority, "someday you will write a book."

Over and over in the years since, I have praised my wise heavenly Father for giving me two years' tutelage under that wonderful woman who possessed the fear of the Lord and taught it to me. I've even thanked him for the Depression which drove us to that place and which at that time undoubtedly forced Julia Larson back into the classroom.

Having described the various virtues of the Proverbs woman, the speaker editorializes in a kind of prologue, telling us at last what has been the secret of her success. First we learn what it was not. "Charms may wane and beauty wither," Moffatt translates. (She may have had those qualities, but if so, they were secondary or derived and not part of the secret formula.) The fear of the Lord is basic and permanent and has been her foundation. This is what motivated even her determination to do her husband good.

What is this quality which recurs so frequently in Scripture? It is usually translated as reverence. And the word "reverence" as it occurs in Hebrews 12:28 is called "modesty and pious care" in the *Amplified Bible*, while "godly fear" is coupled with "awe." The "fear" of God, then, describes our relationship to him. It's not the same as the anxiety, terror, or panic which he intends for us to avoid.

The fear of the Lord is, in fact, the antidote to these other unholy fears. When the people of Israel saw thundering and lightning and smoke and heard the trumpet blast as God gave Moses the Ten Commandments, they were understandably frightened nearly out of their wits. But Moses said to them, "Fear not: for God is come to prove you, and that his fear may be before your faces" (Exodus 20:20).

To those who were afraid of other people, Isaiah said, "Neither fear ye their fear. . . . Sanctify the Lord of hosts himself; and let him be your fear" (Isaiah 8:12, 13).

We receive this quality, as we do so many others, from the Lord himself, for he promised (Jeremiah 32:39, 40) that he would put it in the hearts of his children and that such a condition would be good for them.

I find that the fear of the Lord is more than an emotional state; it's a life-style. When God commanded it, in Deuteronomy 13:4, he linked it with loving the Lord, walking in his ways, keeping his commandments, serving him, and cleaving unto him.

There's a beautiful example of this in the vignette of two doughty women, Shiphrah and Puah. The new Pharaoh, who "knew not Joseph," became greatly distressed about the Hebrew population explosion, which continued in spite of the rigors of cruel slavery. Knowing something about genetics, he called in the medical profession. "Kill all Hebrew boys as soon as they are born," he commanded the midwives, "but . . . let the girls live" (Exodus 1:16, TLB).

But because the midwives feared God, we are told, they did not comply, choosing if necessary to commit suicide rather than infanticide. When Pharaoh called them to account for the continued appearance of male infants, they blamed it on the Hebrew women's rapid delivery system. Shiphrah and Puah must have survived this dereliction of duty only because of God. (Proverbs 10:27 promises that the fear of the Lord will prolong life.)

"So the people of Israel continued to multiply. . . . And because the midwives revered God, he gave them children of their own" (Exodus 1:20, 21, TLB).

Perhaps today we need a healthy reappraisal of this sober virtue. God is not just a great-grandfather who pats us on the head no matter how we behave. Instead, he wishes us to walk carefully ("The fear of the Lord is clean," Psalm 19:9) and to understand his thoughts ("The fear of the Lord is to hate evil," Proverbs 8:13).

To demonstrate this desire, God sent his only Son to be our Example, and then dispatched the Holy Spirit to be our Helper. In Acts 9:31 the fear of the Lord is linked with the comfort of the Holy Ghost.

God promises many benefits to those who fear him: mercy, his delight, and freedom from want. Furthermore, "He fulfills the desires of those who reverence and trust him; he hears their cries for help and rescues them" (Psalm 145:19, TLB).

That promise is beautifully illustrated by something that happened to my friend Kathy after a long period of deep suffering. At 4:00 one morning, God gave her a mental picture of a lamb in the lap of Jesus. It was wearing a blue ribbon.

She wrote, "Then I simply said 'Jesus,' and there he was, filling my heart and thoughts as my loving Shepherd. And there I was, a scrawny, bruised, bleeding, crying little lamb caught in a crevice; I was struggling and unable to get out, too weary to try any more and very much aware of the snarling wolves nearby.

"He reached down and swiftly gathered me up, ever so gently and tenderly. I relaxed as I felt the strength of his arms and the softness of his purple robe.

"Suddenly we were in a serene yet exhilarating and refreshing place. The Shepherd sat down and cradled me in his arms. I could hear water trickling nearby and I could smell a beautiful fragrance.

"He put his one hand under my tired head and with his other hand scooped up a handful of cool, clear water and gave me a drink. I found the words of the Twenty-third Psalm going through my mind, and I felt strengthened.

"As I snuggled in to fall asleep in his lap, these things came to me:

. . . He was the Lamb that was slain for me. He will not permit me to be slain.

. . . He will need to give me a bath, clean my wounds and apply ointment.

. . . I need to just rest in his lap for a time and be hand-fed by him before he will put me back down on the ground to follow closely at his heels.

. . . He has this much time for each child of his, for each sheep of his pasture.

. . . Jesus wants to groom each one of us into a prize-winning, blue-ribbon sheep that hears and obeys his voice."

Kathy's narrative made vivid for me the Lord's statement in Psalm 103:13, "Like as a father pitieth his children, so the Lord pitieth them that fear him," for the Hebrew "pity" means to fondle.

For me, then, to fear the Lord means not only to reverence him, but to consider him and his wishes in every aspect of my life, to cleave unto him.

My friend LaVorris once wrote, "Every step we take he has already stepped in, as we 'follow' him. He's already tried it and found it safe and profitable for us. My, to put my foot in his footstep while the print is still warm!"

As the Proverbs lady succeeded because she feared the Lord, so may we; for this passage goes universal by saying "*a woman*." And the grammar is emphatic. Such a woman *shall* be praised.

All that concerns my husband, my children, my business, or myself will fall into place as I let Jesus Christ "in all things . . . have the preeminence" (Colossians 1:18).

The Lord knows that he has many competitors for first place in my attention. Even as I have been writing this, my thoughts have been besieged by several important concerns. But he has just shown me in Scripture a beautiful new prayer, "Unite my heart to fear thy name" (Psalm 86:11). When my heart is scattered, God will help me "get it all together" and focus it on himself.

Praise and reverence be unto him.

TWENTY-ONE
Let Her Works Praise

*Give her of the fruit of her hands; and let her
own works praise her in the gates.*
Proverbs 31:31

First her children, then her husband, and now the Proverbs
woman's *own accomplishments* praise her. It must not be wrong to
receive recognition and verbal bouquets.

My friend Helen used to say, "Everybody appreciates appreciation!"

There are two parts to our heroine's reward. First she receives
for herself the good things that she has been dispensing to
others, the fruit of her hands. It is interesting to apply the
numerical principle here, too, for this is the seventh mention of
her hands. We know that seven is one of the perfect numbers
and is used throughout the Word to indicate fullness and perfection. Since it often refers to divine completeness, I believe this
passage looks ahead to heavenly rewards.

Some of our rewards do come on earth. Paul asked the Roman
Christians to help Phoebe, who was planning to visit them, in all
possible ways because she had been a helper of many persons,
including himself.

And Jesus promised, "For if you give, you will get!" (Luke
6:38, TLB).

But it's the future hope which is most comforting, for in the
here and now we frequently labor unrewarded, just as Jesus did.
Lots of women have cooked more meals per square casserole for

guests than they will ever get back, or sent more greeting cards than they received, or worked behind the scenes while the "front women" enjoyed the credit.

From the book, *My Thoughts Toward You*, these words offer hope: "It seems that others receive more praise for service rendered. Does this bother you? I have said that much praise given here may be the only praise received. But when works of love go unnoticed by your fellowmen, I never fail to see this and plan for future rewards."[1]

But then comes the grand finale: "Let her own works praise her in the gates." Apparently the gates not only provided the setting for legal decisions and the settling of disputes, but also for awards ceremonies.

So we have a charming picture of her many deeds standing up and shouting, "Let's hear it for the Virtuous Woman!" while they place a diadem of victory upon her head.

Listen, beloved friends: if we fear the Lord, we too *will be praised*. The Lord not only gives us constant encouragement and praise while we live out our lives here, but he is planning a recognition banquet the likes of which we can't even imagine.

He himself will offer the opening fanfare: "On that day the announcement to Jerusalem will be, 'Cheer up, don't be afraid. For the Lord your God has arrived to live among you. . . . He will rejoice over you in great gladness; he will love you and not accuse you.' Is that a joyous choir I hear? No, it is the Lord himself exulting over you in happy song" (Zephaniah 3:16, 17, TLB). And that promise belongs to us, for he has promised to write upon us the name, "New Jerusalem" (Revelation 3:12).

But there's more to come at the gates of the Eternal City. He has arranged testimonials, our own works to praise us. That's not too difficult to imagine concerning our successes:

. . . the Bible studies we taught

. . . foster children mothered

. . . conventions organized which blessed so many

---

[1] From *My Thoughts Toward You*. Copyright © 1975 by PM Publications, Route One, St. Cloud, Minnesota 56301. Used by permission.

... promotions earned without compromising Christian standards

... Christmas pageants with hours spent in making Styrofoam wings, hunting bathrobes, and coaching the head Wise Man *not* to say, "We have found his star in the yeast."

... sacred paintings entered in competitions

... witnessing

... fervent prayers which availed much

God takes note, however, of all that we do in the fear of the Lord (he's a heart monitor, remember?). Some of the things we wrote off as unimportant or as failures will also stand to call us blessed. "Behold! God is mighty, and yet He regards nothing as trivial" (Job 36:5, Berk.):

... tons of dirty dishes washed

... endless errors on papers teachers have red-penciled and sighed over

... stinking dressings nurses peeled from ungrateful patients

... futile efforts of women to preserve ailing marriages

... years of exhausting care of invalid husbands

... hours spent with alcoholic neighbors who returned to their booze

... sincere, off-key singers patiently directed by choir leaders

... lonely nights for business travelers in strange motels

... flowers laid on the graves of husbands and children

He who can count our hairs can also compute our works. We can trust them, when we fear the Lord, to praise us in the gates.

And when we who have endured receive our crowns of life, we will turn, in stately sequence, and cast them at his feet, where they will become the "many crowns" of Jesus Christ, our King of kings and Lord of lords.

Hallelujah! Amen and Amen.